Riding the Internet Highway

Sharon Fisher

NRP
NEW RIDERS
PUBLISHING

New Riders Publishing,
Indianapolis, Indiana

384.3
F-536 r
1993

Riding the Internet Highway

By Sharon Fisher

Published by:
New Riders Publishing
201 W. 103rd Street
Indianapolis, IN 46290 USA

Printed in the United States of America   3 4 5 6 7 8 9 0

Library of Congress Cataloging-in-Publication Data

Fisher, Sharon, 1959-

    Riding the Internet Highway / Sharon Fisher.
        p.   cm.
    Includes index.
    ISBN 1-56205-192-x : $16.95
    1. Internet (Computer network)
    I. Title.
    TK5105.875.I57F57 1993
    384.3—dc20   93-11676

                                         CIP

Publisher
Lloyd J. Short

Associate Publisher
Tim Huddleston

Acquisitions Manager
Cheri Robinson

Acquisitions Editor
Rob Tidrow

Managing Editor
Matthew Morrill

Marketing Manager
Gregg Bushyeager

Product Director
Rob Tidrow

Production Editor
Steve Weiss

Editors
John Kane, Lisa Wilson,
Phil Worthington

Technical Editor
Karen Lynn White

Book Design and Production
Roger Morgan
Juli Pavey
Angela Pozdol
Barbara Webster

Proofreaders
Angela Bannan
Terri Edwards
Linda Koopman
Bob La Roche
Sean Medlock
Tonya R. Simpson
Marcella Thompson
Dennis Wesner

Indexed by
Johnna VanHoose

Acquisitions Coordinator
Stacey Beheler

Editorial Secretary
Karen Opal

Publishing Assistant
Melissa Keegan

About the Author

Sharon Fisher has been using the Internet since 1986, when she got an account on the WELL. Since then, she has used the Internet as a tool both professionally and socially.

Ms. Fisher has been a senior writer for *Communications Week*, where she covers network management, since October, 1991.

Previously, she was a freelance writer for three years, specializing in data communications. Her work has appeared in publications such as *Byte*, *ComputerWorld, InfoWorld, Unix World, Network World, LAN Times, LAN, LAN Technology, MacWorld, MacUser, PC World, Datamation*, and *Software*.

Before that, she was senior editor, communications, for *InfoWorld*. She has also written data communications manuals for Hewlett-Packard Co.

In the non-computer area, her work has appeared in the *Columbia Journalism Review* and *Diablo Business*.

She has also contributed to three books: *The PC LAN Primer, Using Enable 2nd Edition*, and *Windows 3.1 Revealed*.

Ms. Fisher holds a B.S. in computer science from Rensselaer Polytechnic Institute and is a graduate of the Stanford Publishing Course.

She can be reached via the Internet at `slf@netcom.com`.

Acknowledgements

This book could not have been written without the Internet itself, which put me in contact with many fine people who helped, and many others who offered. Thanks, in no particular order, go to the following persons:

Eric Theiese, for assistance with Chapter 5.

Jean-Marie Diaz ("Ambar"), for introducing me to MUDs and draping me with kittens.

Erik Fair, for general assistance but most especially with Chapter 2.

Rich Pixley, for being supportive when I needed that and for beating on me when I needed that, too.

Rob Tidrow and Steve Weiss, from New Riders Publishing, for their encouragement and support.

Karen Lynn White, for her invaluable assistance and input as technical editor.

John Kane, Lisa Wilson, and Phil Worthington for their dedicated work as copy editors.

Jeff Herman, for being my Very First Agent.

Desiree at Netcom for arranging a test account.

Tim Wilson and David Buerger, my editors at *Communications Week*, for being flexible and supportive.

Trademark Acknowledgments

Table of Contents

Welcome to This Book!

Obviously you are a person of intelligence and fine literary discernment. :-) (This is a smiley. They live on the Internet, among other places. You will learn more about smileys later.)

The Internet is everywhere, and it's not just for geeks anymore. President Clinton and Vice President Gore are on the Internet. Musicians are on the Internet, and promote that fact on their album covers. Cartoonists are on the Internet, and reference the Internet in their work—and do not feel the need to explain the reference.

But perhaps most significantly, *business* is on the Internet. As the computer age heads toward the end of the century, commercial interests on the Internet are growing at an exponential rate. Business applications on the Internet are booming and the spoils of commercial success certainly won't go to the technologically naive user.

You have probably picked up this book because you want to learn more about that world. You might even be ready to join those who are using the Internet, and are looking for a guide. This book may be it. What are your needs?

Why This Book is Different

If you are looking for the be-all and end-all book to describe everything up-to-the-minute about the Internet, this book is not for you. In fact, the book you want does not exist; the Internet is changing so fast that it is difficult for anything other than the Internet itself to keep up with the constant state of change.

If you are looking for a book to tell you how to buy and install a modem and communications software, and then use the Internet, this book is not for you, either. There are many wonderful books that cover this and other basic hardware/software topics; this is not one of them.

In fact, if you have never used CompuServe, a local bulletin-board system, or some other on-line service, you might want to do that first. This will get you accustomed to your communications software, modem, and on-line culture before venturing out among the millions of Internet users. If you were learning to drive, you would most likely not do so on the interstate at rush hour; similarly, there are more appropriate places to get on-line for the first time than the Internet.

What this book does provide is this: a basic introduction, for PC or Macintosh users, to the main features of the Internet, including electronic mail, file transfer, Usenet conferencing software, and search tools. This book does not cover each area in exhaustive detail because, more than likely, you do not *need* that level of detail. Perhaps you have looked at other books on the Internet and found them too in-depth, presuming a level of previous knowledge and areas of interest that you do not have.

However, this book does point you to various sources along the way—generally available on the Internet itself—to help you learn more about those areas that intrigue you. In the meantime, this book will help you *use* the Internet without having to devote a lot of study to it.

The 80-20 rules says that 20 percent of the information provides 80 percent of the value; the goal of this book is to be that 20 percent.

The Organization of This Book

This book consists of five chapters and five appendices.

Chapter 1 is an introduction to the Internet, including how to find an Internet access provider and get an account.

Chapter 2, "Connecting with Other Individuals," covers electronic mail and mailing lists, which allow you to communicate with other people directly.

Chapter 3, "Connecting with Other Computers," covers remote logging in to other machines on the Internet, both to use resources there and to transfer files back to your own Internet system.

Chapter 4, "Using Netnews," covers Usenet, a conferencing system that is widespread on the Internet.

Chapter 5, "Finding Information on the Internet," covers the new generation of Internet tools, which search the Internet to find information for you.

Appendices include the PDIAL list of public access Unix providers; the National Science Foundation Network Acceptable Use Policy; a list of country codes to help you identify non-U.S. sites; a dictionary of "smileys," those odd typographic conventions that on-line denizens use to convey emotion (these are addictive; if you are like most on-line users, you will find yourself inserting them in handwritten text as well); and a whois servers list, giving you telephone directory-like access to millions of other Internet users.

Conventions Used in this Book

It is always difficult to differentiate between explanation and instruction; without typographic conventions, it is sometimes not clear what is supposed to be typed in and what is description.

To help in that process, this book uses a number of typographic conventions:

Text that represents user input is printed `in this font`.

Text that represents computer screen output is printed `in this font`.

Commands that appear in body text are printed **in this font**.

In both user input or screen output, variables are printed *in italics*, along with the respective `input` or `output` font. A *variable* simply means that the information you will see or need to type is specific to you and not actually what appears on the printed page. If you see a command to type *username*, for example, that means to type your own name.

Text that is marked for emphasis or for titles is printed *in this font*.

In addition, this book contains numerous screen diagrams taken from actual Internet sessions.

A Final Word

The thing to remember most about the Internet is that it really comes down to people. E-mail puts you in contact with other people directly; Netnews helps you find other people; even the files that you transfer are created by people. The Internet is nothing magical; it is just another way to keep in touch with people. But perhaps that is magical after all.

CHAPTER 1

Introduction to the Internet

In the same way that you would want to know something about the freeway system before driving your car onto it, you need to know about the Internet before connecting your PC or Macintosh to it.

You would not want to drive your car onto the freeway without knowing where the road led, whether it would take you to your destination, whether your car could keep up with the speed of traffic, or what the "rules of the road" were.

This chapter will give you that information. It will cover:

➡ Examples of the ways you can use the Internet

➡ How the Internet came to exist

➡ What hardware and software your PC needs to be able to link to the Internet

➡ How to find an Internet site

➡ How to set up an Internet account, using a real-life example

➡ How to act courteously on the Internet

→ A very basic list of Unix commands you will need to know

→ How to protect your PC, the data on it, and the data on your Internet accounts

What is the Internet?

The Internet is a giant network of computers located all over the world that communicate with each other. At various stops on the highway, there are "sights"—similarly, at various places on the Internet, there are repositories of software and other information that you can download for free. This is called *file transfer*.

A WORD ABOUT THE TERM "PC"

"PC" will be used throughout this book to represent all kinds of personal computers. When something specific to a particular type of PC arises, the text will say so—for example, "On the Macintosh," or "On an IBM-compatible PC running Microsoft Windows."

The Internet also gets you places in a hurry. You can send a message electronically to a user across the country or around the world, and it will get there in seconds. This is called electronic mail, or *e-mail*. You can also call up an Internet computer local to yourself and *log in* to that computer, and then use the Internet to jump to another computer on the Internet that perhaps has other resources you would like to use. This is called *remote login*.

And you can meet people along the road, leaving them messages on electronic 'bulletin boards' as you go. This is called *Netnews*.

Some Brief Internet History...

Originally, the Internet was set up by government and research institutions so that they could communicate with each other. But people on it soon learned how useful—and fun!—it was to communicate with each other, and more and more people started to get onto the Internet.

As the Internet became more popular, commercial organizations began offering access to the Internet so that you did not have to be a researcher to get an Internet account. As a result the Internet became more organized and easier to use, like the highway system.

...and a Brief Word of Friendly Advice

But you wouldn't want to drive your car onto the freeway without knowing where the road led, whether it would take you to your destination, whether your car could keep up with the speed of traffic, or what the "rules of the road" were.

This book will assume that you are already familiar with logging onto on-line services, such as CompuServe or a local bulletin board system (BBS). If you are not, however, you might want to start practicing there first.

What the Internet Can Provide and Its Growth

You may already have a reason for wanting to be on the Internet, even if it is simple curiosity about what sort of resources are there. This "information highway" is becoming an increasingly important resource to all kinds of people—not just highly technical engineers and scientists. And as the Internet grows, it becomes even more important for you to get an Internet connection, in the same way that the use of telephones reached critical mass earlier in this century.

What You Can Use the Internet For

The Internet itself is both the thousands of computers on it and the greater physical connection linking them. But what probably matters to you is not the computers themselves, or even their links—which may well be transparent to most users—but what you can do once you get going *on* the Internet. While you might go on a Sunday drive sometime, where the purpose is simply to enjoy the drive, generally "getting there is half the fun" does not apply to the Internet.

A Small World of Communication

For example, you can use your Internet connection to communicate with others, both people you already know and ones you've yet to meet. If your sister is going to school, and you somehow never get around to writing her a letter, and your conflicting schedules make exchanging telephone calls difficult, you can log onto your Internet host and create an electronic letter, or *electronic mail,* that will be sent to her in a matter of minutes.

EXACTLY WHAT IS ELECTRONIC MAIL?

Electronic mail means that you create a file that contains a note or letter, and then you send it to the recipient's electronic *mailbox,* where he or she can read it. It is like a fax, except that it goes directly into the recipient's computer rather than into a fax machine. Instead, one computer sends the electronic mail directly to the other one, via the Internet.

Or if you have learned that a historian in a foreign country is working in an area you find interesting, you can drop that person a line, asking about his research and whether he can point you to other information in the area.

The recipients of your e-mail can then read it at their convenience and can reply to you automatically. They can also forward your e-mail to someone else, save it for their records, or do both.

The Global Party Line

Sometimes a group of people interested in a specific subject set up a *mailing list* just to discuss that topic. And in the same way that a postal or company mailing list sends paper copies of messages to all specified parties, an e-mail mailing list helps the sender reach a target audience through their PCs. That way, groups of people separated by time or distance can discuss a project or an interest and even arrange to meet when they happen to be in each other's areas. For example, science fiction fans often set up parties at the major "sci-fi" conventions so they can meet the people they have been talking to for months (and sometimes years).

In addition, some Internet sites allow you to communicate with another person in *real time*—that is, the two of you are both on your respective Internet connections at the same time, and you exchange information much as you would in a phone call, except that you are each typing it in on your computers. This is called *chat, talk*, or *IRC*, for Internet Relay Chat.

LET YOUR FINGERS DO THE TALKING

TIP

Internet Relay Chats (IRCs) enable two or more people at separate PCs to "talk" to each other in real time. *Real time* just means it's live with no delays. And instead of speaking over a telephone, you're type-talking between your keyboards.

Having an Internet connection offers other benefits as well. Once you are logged in to any computer on the Internet, you can then remotely connect to any other computer on the Internet (assuming you have the authorization to do so). For example, if you are traveling and want to check your e-mail back home, you can call in to a local Internet node, log in there, and then log on from there to the Internet node you normally use, all without paying long-distance telephone charges there.

Information: Internet's Free Commodity

Also, if you have used other on-line services, such as CompuServe or local bulletin boards, you know that they can be fabulous repositories for free software and other data. The Internet is home to hundreds of such sites, which offer goodies ranging from software for your PC or Macintosh to weather predictions to data from the U.S. government. And all of it is free, without the download charges that some on-line systems such as CompuServe impose.

Many machines on the Internet, and even some that aren't (which will be discussed later), offer a way to communicate publicly with others who are interested in a particular topic. This lane of the electronic highway is called *news*, *Netnews*, or *Usenet*, after the name of the network for transmitting news.

For example, have you ever had a question but didn't know where to start looking for the answer? ("Does anyone know the words to the Bugs Bunny theme song?") Netnews not only offers you places to ask, but you might get an answer within a matter of minutes. And once you establish contacts in this way, you can communicate with them privately using e-mail as well.

Of course, questions do not have to be trivial (sorry, Bugs). You can also ask about how to get a particular piece of hardware or software to work, how best to set up your corporate network, or where to get a job. You can find out what vendors to patronize— and to avoid. Many companies—not just ones in the computer field, either—offer access to the Internet because it provides such a wide field of people to use as business resources.

The History of the Internet

What we know today as the Internet began in the late 1960s as a project from the Advanced Research Projects Agency (ARPA) of the U.S. Department of Defense. It was an experimental network intended to allow scientists receiving research grants from ARPA to communicate with each other. Consequently, the network became known as the *ARPAnet*.

Members of the ARPAnet community soon realized that they used the network for much more than discussing research. The physicist in California who talked about linear accelerators might

also be interested in that new television series, "Star Trek."
Several Star Trek fans might then discover a mutual interest in
philosophy, computers, or mountain climbing. And as more
people learned about the benefits of nearly instantaneous electronic communication, the number of people wanting to get on
the ARPAnet grew.

In the late 1980s, the National Science Foundation (NSF) funded
an upgrade for the ARPAnet, to be called the *NSFnet*. It was
intended to link a dozen supercomputer centers around the
United States with high-speed lines that could transmit up to 1.5
million bits per second *(mbps)* of data with an eventual upgrade
planned to support up to 45 mbps.

In addition, the plan called for a number of *regional networks* to
be linked to the NSFnet. If NSFnet was the equivalent to the U.S.
interstate highway system, the regional networks were the
equivalent to state highway systems. And in a new development
for the Net (Internet's nickname), which had always been funded
by the government, some of the regional networks began selling
accounts to ordinary people and businesses, not just those with
government research contracts.

The Internet Today

Today, the Internet is so large and complex, as shown in figure
1.1, that nobody knows exactly how many computers are on it,
much less how many users are on it. Certainly the number of
users is in the millions. Since the late 1980s, data traffic on the
Internet has grown at a rate of 20 percent per month, an increase
dramatically reflected in NSFnet membership as well, as shown in
figure 1.2.

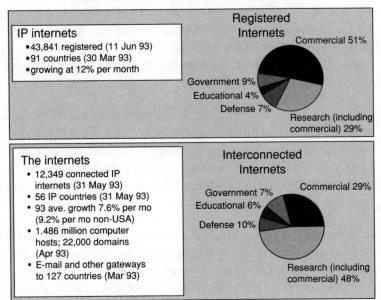

Figure 1.1:

A simplification of
what the Internet
looks like today.

How the Internet Fits Together

Some people find it hard to understand exactly how the Internet
fits together because we often tend to view things as a pyramid or
inverted tree structure with control being imposed from above.
Nothing could be further from the truth when dealing with the
Internet, which is composed of thousands of autonomous LANs
(Local Area Networks) connected by redundant channels.

Think of It as a Biological System

It is easier to understand the Internet structure if you compare it
to a biological system. Each cell or functioning unit continues to
do its own thing while maintaining some communication with
other cells or computer groupings in the unit. Just as no one cell
in your body keeps track of what all the others are doing, no one
computer can know exactly who or how many other computers
and computer systems find connections to the structure. At the
same time, other computers lose their connections and are no
longer part of the Internet.

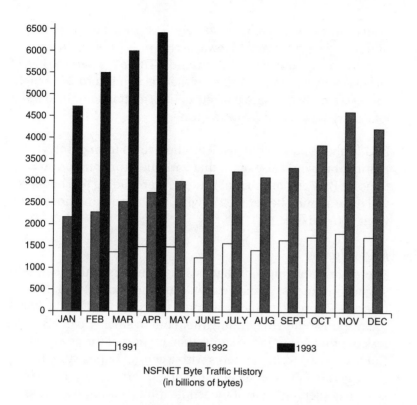

1991 1992 1993

NSFNET Byte Traffic History
(in billions of bytes)

Figure 1.2:

The rise in Internet-related NSFnet use.

Redundancy Means Internet Has You Covered

The Internet has a great deal of *redundancy* built in. Although there may be only one connection from your PC to another computer, all of the larger computers routing mail have many connections. This redundancy is important to the functioning of the Internet. If a machine or group of machines are down for some reason, Internet continues to function as communication routes or detours are built on the fly around any missing computers.

Or Think of It as a Transport Stysytem

Another way to look at this is to view Internet not just as a highway, but as an entire transportation system crisscrossing the entire world. Don't think of the Internet as just one highway with limited access points, but as all highways, all with many access roads, all connected to many others. There are paths of many different sizes from the driveways used only by a few to the superhighways traveled by thousands. There are parking lots of almost every size located all over the place. If Internet is a highway system, the cars are packets of information and the parking lots are repositories of information.

In this book you will not just learn how to go from point A to point B, but you'll also learn that with the proper map you can get to point B by any number of routes. After reading this book, you will have a much better idea of what is available and how to find what you can use.

How It All Stays Together

There is a managing unit that assigns numbers to the central or larger computer systems that make up the backbone of the Internet. There, identifying numbers are given out in blocks and the responsibility for handing them out in smaller parcels is the task of other computer systems that are part of the group. Unlike Compuserve or other systems with a central billing system, nobody is truly in charge of managing Internet. Because no one system is keeping track of the whole thing, it is impossible to say how many computers are part of the Internet at any one time. It would be even more difficult to estimate how many users are part of it.

Data sent from one site to another can take any of a number of different routes along the way. In general, this is completely transparent to the user, much the way that routing U.S. mail is transparent—it goes into the box or post office, and gets delivered to the recipient, who neither knows nor cares what route the letter took to get there (just that it gets where it's supposed to go).

In fact, different parts of the same electronic message may travel over different Internet routes to adjust for network traffic. Because this happens seemingly invisibly to you, this is an example of *transparent* technology.

A Look Inside the Electronic Postal System

There is no central post office location for the Internet where some all-knowing machine keeps track of all the addresses in use. Instead, each routing computer keeps a partial listing found from return addresses. Information is sent in packets, not letters.

For example, let's say a computer located in Michigan gets a packet from California that came from a computer in Iowa. If there is space in a special table or if the volume of packets from California is high enough, then the computer in Michigan will note the fact that mail to California can be sent back to this machine in Iowa that knows how to connect to California. Notice there that each address isn't kept, only the first hop that must be made.

The next time a user sends a packet to California, the routing computer will send it to the computer in Iowa. Of course, every routing computer will have a place to send any packet it doesn't know what to do with. Usually this default will be a bigger computer that will be keeping track of more information. For this mail system to work, things must happen very quickly. Packets are shipped out almost as soon as they come in. If the packet isn't at the right location, it is passed to another computer and never stored for any length of time.

Each routing computer treats packets of information that don't belong at that location as hot potatoes that must be given to another as soon as possible. The potatoes may not take a direct route but eventually they will land at a routing computer that sends them to the place they need to go. Packets also die or are passed over after a certain number of hops or after a certain number of days, so that old information does not hang around forever.

Just as a post office doesn't guarantee that every letter will get through, the Internet will occasionally lose a bit of information. The system is called a *best effort delivery*. Because the system tolerates a few fumbles, a much greater volume can be sent in very little time.

How Far Has the Internet Come?

Not so many years ago, e-mail routing was very different; some-one wishing to send an e-mail message not only needed to know the recipient's electronic address, but the most efficient way to get there as well. And the most efficient way might not be the shortest way; the knowledgeable Internet user knew which connections were fast and which were slow and how often messages were transmitted and when. For example, the shortest electronic route between San Francisco and Berkeley, both in northern California, might be through Carnegie-Mellon Univer-sity in Pittsburgh, simply because of how frequently one com-puter dialed another and the speed of the connections between them.

In addition to increasing the size and complexity of its network in the U.S., the Internet is building its connections to other networks in the world as well. Today, you can electronically travel far and wide, from Antarctica to Amsterdam, Alabama to Australia.

How far has it come? You could get e-mail to Russia since shortly before the fall of the Iron Curtain. You can get firsthand knowlege of the war in Bosnia. You can get to any location where the technology is supported. In fact, if you can make a call out of the country and have access to resources eleswhere, you don't need official sanction from the ruling government. Internet transends political borders.

INTERNET: SUPPORT IN HIGH PLACES

And the Internet will keep growing. Part of the platform used by candidates Bill Clinton and Al Gore in the 1992 presidential campaign was a proposal called the National Research and Education Network, or NREN, which Gore had originally spon-sored as a senator.

What this all means to you is simply this: More than likely, somewhere near you, there is a way for you to get on the Internet. Perhaps it will be through your job. Perhaps it could be through a course at a local university. Perhaps it will be through purchasing an account on a local commercial system that belongs to the Internet. But somewhere you should be able to get an account. An "account," like a charge account, lets you accumulate charges that are then billed to you. Some accounts go by a flat fee, while others are usage-based, such as having a per-minute charge. The account is also what provides you with an identity on the Internet.

What Your PC or Mac Needs to Link to the Internet

Your PC itself will not be on the Internet. Rather, you will use your PC to dial in to a local machine that is on the Internet, as shown in figure 1.3, and communicate with that machine from your PC in the same way that you use your PC to dial in to any other online service, such as CompuServe or a local bulletin board.

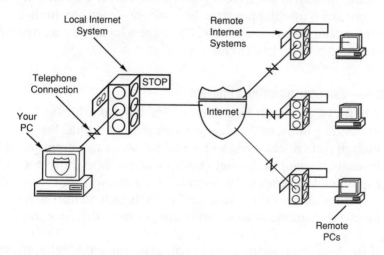

Figure 1.3:
The relationship between your PC and the Internet.

To communicate with your local Internet host, you will need both *hardware* and *software*.

Hardware—Your Modem

A modem is a piece of hardware that translates the PC's digital signals into analog signals that can be transmitted over a telephone line. Your local Internet machine—in other words, the Internet machine, generally in your geographic area, on which you have an account and which you use as your "on-ramp" to the Internet—will also have a modem. This modem will translate the analog signals back to the digital.

You will need to check with your Internet account provider to see whether they have any restrictions on the type of modem you have. For example, some Internet account providers only support a particular type of modem or may charge extra for high-speed modems.

If you have a reasonably standard 1200- or 2400-bps modem that you have used successfully to communicate with other online services, you are not likely to have any problems.

Again, your local Internet provider should be able to let you know about any particular points to be aware of—such as whether high-speed access is available. Choosing a local Internet provider is discussed later in this chapter.

Software—Your Communications Program

When a PC logs onto an online service, it usually does so by pretending to be, or *emulating*, a computer terminal. Even though you are not using a terminal per se, many computers that let multiple people use them traditionally refer to those people's capabilities in terms of "terminals," the same way that a car still measures power in "horsepower" even though no horses are involved. Communications software performs this function.

If you have been logging onto another online service already, you most likely already have, and are familiar with, a communications software package for your PC.

Examples of communications software include Crosstalk, ProComm, and White Knight.

The types of tasks that you will be able to perform on the Internet will depend on what sort of terminal the communications software can emulate. Therefore, when you create your account on the local Internet system, you will most likely be asked what kind of terminal you have. For example, one of the most basic, widely supported kinds of terminals is *TTY*, or teletype. If you choose to emulate this kind of terminal—a lowest-common-denominator— you are likely to have little trouble finding an Internet system that knows how to talk to this kind of terminal.

On the other hand, if your communications software *only* lets you emulate this very basic kind of terminal, you may find that you cannot run some of the more sophisticated e-mail and Netnews programs on the Internet node.

To run most of the typical programs on the Internet machines, you need to emulate a *VT-100* terminal. The VT-100 is manufactured and sold by Digital Equipment Corp.; it has become an industry standard and as so, is widely used. Check your communications software or manual to see if the program will let your PC emulate the VT-100. Then see what changes you will need to make in your program as it is set up now to accomplish that. (You may well find that your PC has been emulating a VT-100 terminal all along.) If you are connecting through a local university you will probably log into a university computer that is part of the Net.

To check out what sorts of terminal emulation your communications software provides, check the software manual's index or table of contents under "Terminal Emulation" to see what is available.

Additional Hardware and Software Options

With a modem and basic communications software, you have all the equipment you need to communicate between your PC and a local Internet node. However, additional programs are available for your PC that can make the Internet easier to use. These programs are called *front ends*. They may be generic packages, some of which you can download for free from the Internet, or they may be specific to your local Internet site.

WHAT IS DOWNLOADING?

To "download" means to copy data from a system on the Internet to your PC. Similarly, "upload" means to copy data from your PC to a system on the Internet.

For example, the WELL, an Internet site in Sausalito, California, offers Sweeper. This free software, developed by WELL user Jim Rutt, enables your PC to automatically perform functions such as reading your e-mail. Sweeper works only with the WELL.

Unfortunately, most of these programs are intended to be used by more sophisticated users over a local area network or through more complex dial-up connections.

YOU, TOO, CAN BE AN INTERNET PROVIDER

With more sophisticated software—which you can often download for free from the Internet—and with the cooperation of a local Internet node, you could even set up your own PC to be an Internet node by itself. Advantages of this include keeping control of data the Internet provides—for example, you might wish to keep Netnews postings around longer than a commercial Internet provider can handle. You can also become an Internet provider yourself and give friends or family accounts on your machine. In addition, the more sophisticated tools help you use the Internet more efficiently, such as by providing an easier to use interface to Netnews. However, the details of how to do so are beyond the scope of this book.

How to Find an Internet Account

The easiest way to get an account on the Internet is through your job or through school (a few high schools and many universities are on the Internet). Many companies, even ones not in the computer industry, have Internet connections these days. Start with your local MIS (Management Information System) department. The advantage of such an account is that it is likely to be free to the user.

You should be aware, though, that some companies and universities limit the types of access that they grant to their accounts. For example, some companies require that any Internet use must be work-related, which is fine if you want to talk about your job, but will not work if you want to talk about astrology. Similarly, some companies and universities do not get a full feed of Netnews, meaning you could miss out on a large number of Netnews groups.

If you cannot get an account through your job or school, then you will need to find a commercially available account, most likely through what is called a *public access Unix system.*

Having "Access" vs. Being "On" the Internet

Before you find and sign up for an Internet account, you need to know that Internet terminology is not necessarily clear on a couple of factors. One of these is the aspect of being "on" the Internet. For example, many computers can exchange e-mail and Netnews without necessarily being "on" the Internet. Instead, these machines telephone another machine on the Internet at periodic intervals and exchange e-mail and Netnews at those intervals. In other words, there are different levels of Internet access—like having associate memberships and full memberships to organizations—and Internet providers are not always clear about what levels of access they provide.

One example of such a link is known as a uucp feed. The term *uucp* stands for Unix-to-Unix CoPy and is the name of the software as well as the communications method used to set up this kind of link. But if you get an account on a machine that only has a uucp connection, you will not be able to perform some Internet functions, such as remotely logging in to other machines on the Internet.

Consequently, when you are looking at your various options, you need to consider what functions you actually need and whether the public accounts in your area can provide these functions. Perhaps all you actually need is e-mail and Netnews, and you do not expect to log in to other systems. Systems offering this type of account may be more common in your area, or less expensive; in fact, you may have such access already. For example, on CompuServe you can send and receive e-mail to and from people with Internet accounts.

Finding a Commercial Internet Account

You can find a local, commercial Internet account the same way that you can find out about any bulletin board system. Ask your friends. Check in your local computer store or user group meeting. Look in both national and local computer publications.

In northern California, for example, you can find two free local computer magazines: *Microtimes*, published monthly, and *Computer Currents*, published biweekly. Both of them run extensive lists of bulletin board systems. Look through those lists for indicators such as "public access Unix system" or "Internet access."

(Your local computer magazine, if there is one, is often your *best* source in general for local bulletin board information; while national magazines occasionally publish such lists, they are far from complete.)

In addition, several lists of public access Unix systems are posted every month or so as Netnews postings and can be downloaded from several sites. Granted, if you do not have access to the Internet, you will not be able to read these lists. But perhaps a friend has access and can print off a copy for you.

In addition, Appendix A shows PDIAL, one of the most extensive of these lists. You can check these lists for services in your area code that provide the types of Internet and other features you want.

HOW TO GET YOUR OWN PDIAL LIST

So how do you get the PDIAL list from the Internet if you do not already have an Internet account? Well, it is sort of like getting your first job when you have no experience. Sometimes these lists are posted on other on-line services. Or perhaps you have a friend with Internet access who can get a copy of the list for you.

For example, most public access Internet systems require that you have a credit card, to which charges will be billed. However, some will allow you to pay by check or money order. If you do not have, or do not wish to use, a credit card, you will need to look for one of these services.

GETTING HELP FROM THE WELL

If you cannot find an Internet provider in your area code but you do have a CompuServe Packet Network (CPN) node in your area, you might consider the WELL (Whole Earth 'Lectronic Link), a public access Unix and conferencing system. (To find out the closest CPN number to you, call 1-800-848-8980. This is a voice call.)

Though the WELL is in Sausalito, California, it has a contract with CPN whereby users from around the world can log in for a charge of $4 to $12 per hour, in addition to the WELL's regular charge of $10 per month and $2 per hour. Depending on what long-distance charges might be to the nearest Internet provider, the WELL may be more economical through CPN rather than by dialing long-distance.

To use this method, dial your local CPN node, press Enter, and type WELL at the Host Name: prompt. You do not need a CompuServe account to be able to do this. To find a local CPN node, call 1-800-848-8199 and ask. Or, if you know one number and want to look up numbers for other areas, dial your local CPN node and type PHONES at the Host Name: prompt.

Another way to reduce long distance charges is through PC Pursuit. *PC Pursuit* is a telephone service that provides low-cost access to 44 cities. If you are trying to reach an Internet provider in one of those cities, PC Pursuit can reduce your online charges.

The disadvantage is that PC Pursuit lines can often be busy, and it is available only between 6 p.m. and 7 a.m. during the week, as well as all weekend. The service costs $30 for 30 hours, or $50 for 60 hours during this time; otherwise, it costs $10.50 per hour. There is also a $30 registration fee.

For more information on PC Pursuit, and to register, call 1-800-736-1130.

Please note that this information can change rapidly; you should act accordingly. If the service no longer operates and the telephone number has been reassigned, a new customer will not appreciate being awakened at night by a modem tone.

Setting Up an Internet Account

As a basic example, this book will use Netcom, a public access Unix provider in northern California which also provides local access as far north as Seattle and as far south as Los Angeles. Netcom provides full Internet access, including more than 3,000 Netnews groups.

From somewhere—perhaps a friend gave you one of the lists of public access Unix providers—you learn about Netcom. Many services, including Netcom, are set up to provide information to potential new users if they log on as guest. So, set your communications software to dial the Netcom access number closest to you, which for this example will be 415-985-5650.

As you can see from the list in Appendix A, some of the entries will tell you how to set the data parameters. The entry for Netcom, however, does not. For the data parameters for Netcom, or any other system for which you don't have this information, set your communications program to 8,N,1. If that does not work, try 7,E,1.

LINE BUSY? BE PATIENT!

Like any other bulletin board system, a public access Unix system can often be busy, especially during evening and weekend hours. Unfortunately, there really is no way around this other than to use different hours and to keep trying.

When your computer makes the connection to Netcom, Netcom will respond with the information shown in figure 1.4. At the netcom3 login: prompt, type **guest**, press Enter, and then press Enter again to enter a blank at the Password: prompt.

Note that you typed guest in all lowercase. This is common on the Internet and on most Unix systems—they are *case-sensitive*, meaning that Guest would not be the same thing as guest.

Netcom will then ask you for your terminal type. As mentioned earlier in this chapter, this is most commonly VT-100, and you should have configured your communications software to support this type if it is available. Select the appropriate terminal type, and press Enter again. Netcom will show you the screen in figure 1.5.

```
Dialing netcom sf

CONNECT 2400

netcom3 login: guest
Password:
```

```
ALT-F10  HELP | ANSI-BBS | FDX | 2400 N81 | LOG CLOSED | PRT OFF | CR | CR
```

Figure 1.4:

The Netcom login screen.

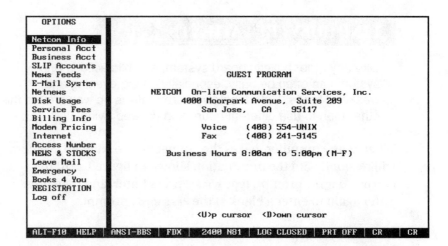

```
OPTIONS

Netcom Info
Personal Acct
Business Acct
SLIP Accounts
News Feeds
E-Mail System
Netnews
Disk Usage
Service Fees
Billing Info
Modem Pricing
Internet
Access Number
NEWS & STOCKS
Leave Mail
Emergency
Books 4 You
REGISTRATION
Log off
```

```
                    GUEST PROGRAM

        NETCOM  On-line Communication Services, Inc.
               4000 Moorpark Avenue,  Suite 209
                  San Jose,   CA    95117

                   Voice    (408) 554-UNIX
                   Fax      (408) 241-9145

          Business Hours 8:00am to 5:00pm (M-F)



              <U>p cursor   <D>own cursor
```

```
ALT-F10  HELP | ANSI-BBS | FDX | 2400 N81 | LOG CLOSED | PRT OFF | CR | CR
```

Figure 1.5:

The Netcom guest screen.

As you can see, one of the entries is Personal Account, which gives you information about what an account for an individual on Netcom provides. Other entries provide information such as telephone access numbers. Netcom does not charge for this information, and neither will most other public access Unix sites, so it is a good idea to read on and get as much information as you can about the service.

HOW TO SAVE SERVICE INFORMATION

You may want to open the capture buffer (or create a log file using your communications software) to save a copy of this information on your PC's hard disk or on a floppy disk. This will let you keep copies of the information, which is handy if you are trying to compare multiple services; you can then refer to them later. In addition, if you are dialed in long distance, or if you are concerned about tying up the telephone line and preventing other users from logging in, simply saving the information to disk and reading it later helps minimize the time you spend logged in.

Before you actually start to register your account, whether it is on Netcom or on any other system, note that you will need a *login ID* and *password*. The login ID, also known as *username*, will be, more or less, your Internet identity, and it can be difficult to change once set up. What do you want it to be? Your first name? Your initials? A nickname? Internet users can have the disconcerting habit of referring to you by your login ID rather than your name, so choose carefully. Also, have a couple of alternatives handy in case your first choice is taken—no doubt there is already a "Pete" on that local Internet system.

Similarly, you will most likely need to enter a password, which will be the "key" to your Internet account, though in some cases the Internet system will provide one for you. If you choose it, remember that it needs to be complex enough to not be easily guessed, yet easy enough for you to remember without writing it down. For more information on choosing passwords, see "Protecting Your Internet Account—Choosing a Password" in the "Security" section of this chapter.

ACCESS IS QUICK—JUST NOT IMMEDIATE

In most cases, even for free accounts, you should not count on being able to use your account for Internet access immediately. Your credit card may need to be verified, your check may need to clear, or you may have to receive a manual through the mail first. Moreover, you may need to read and sign a form explaining the service's Internet access policies before you can perform some functions, such as being allowed to post Netnews or sending e-mail beyond your local machine.

When you are ready to create your Netcom account—either within this session, or perhaps in a later session after you have read and understood the information on Netcom—you can then select the Registration option to begin the process. Netcom then displays the screen shown in figure 1.6.

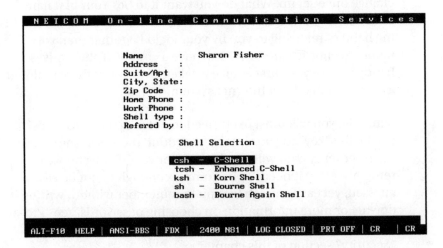

Figure 1.6:

The Netcom registration screen.

Most of the information requested on this screen will be fairly obvious to you—name, address, and so on. But what is shell type?

Remember that most public access Internet accounts are on Unix computer systems. Unix systems offer a number of different ways to communicate with the operating system, and these different ways are known as *shells*. The equivalent, on your IBM-compatible PC, would be "DOS" or "Windows" or "Desqview."

When you have entered the registration information up to this point, Netcom then offers you a list of several Unix shells: csh, tcsh, ksh, sh, and bash. You will note that csh is highlighted. That means that csh is the *default*, or the setting that Netcom will use unless you specify something different. In the same way that VT-100 is the most typical terminal type, the most typical Unix shell is csh. That setting is likely to be the most common one used there, and the one with which the employees will be most familiar, should you have questions later.

When you are confronted with this question, no matter which Internet provider you're using, first try skipping over it to invoke the default for that system. If that does not work, type **csh**. And again, it is important to use all lowercase letters.

Another good question that might not be clear is why Netcom wants to know whom you were referred by? Perhaps just for their records—for example, to find out which of their advertisements was the most successful. Or, they may offer rewards to people who refer other users to the system. The WELL, for example, offers users a $10 credit if new users cite them as a referral. So if a system asks you how you heard of the system, go ahead and tell them.

Next, Netcom will ask you how you intend to pay for the service, and, if you select credit card, will prompt you for your credit card number and expiration date, which you should then type in. In Netcom's case, you enter each block of numbers on your card, and then press Enter after each block.

Some systems, including Netcom, allow you to be billed and then you pay by check. What the user should do depends on their own options and preferences—for example, if they have no credit cards, they will need to find a system that does not require them.

After you indicate how you will pay, Netcom asks what you would like your login ID to be and will tell you if that ID is already in use. You will also be prompted for your password, and Netcom will make sure you use a mix of upper- and lowercase letters and non-alphabetic characters by refusing to accept a password without these characteristics. These characteristics make your password more difficult to guess, in case someone tries to break into your account.

After you have entered this information, if you have used a credit card, Netcom displays a screen to tell you that, for your protection, someone from Netcom will call to confirm before setting up your account. Netcom then returns you to the main guest screen.

Congratulations. You are now on the Internet!

Rules of the Road

But before you start using the Internet, you should be aware of some of the conventions for behavior. If you are trying to meet people or get information, then it is important to make a good first impression—and because the Internet is so large, it is far too easy to make a bad one.

What can make this difficult is that the conventions are not written down anywhere, and different people have different conceptions of what those conventions should be. Moreover, sometimes Internet users only pay lip service to the rules.

Acceptable Use Policies

Some sections of the Internet, particularly those funded by the NSF, have what is known as an *acceptable use policy* on the sorts of things you can use the Internet for. Though technically, data transmitted by these sections of the network must have some scientific or research purpose, in practice it means that overtly commercial messages are frowned upon. The acceptable use policy is shown in Appendix B.

But given that routing of network traffic is transparent to the user, as discussed earlier in "The Internet Today" section, how can a user tell whether a message will travel over the NSFnet portion of the network—where an acceptable use policy is in force—or another portion, where any use is acceptable? For this reason, some industry watchers expect acceptable use policies to eventually be thrown out. At the very least, they are seldom enforced unless users complain, and the offense has to be particularly egregious before much is likely to happen.

What acceptable use boils down to is this: First, check with your Internet provider—starting with the manual—to see if the service has any restrictions on the sorts of ways you can use the Internet. For example, a university may have more restrictions on use than a commercial Internet provider. Ask if the Internet provider has an acceptable use policy or any other particular rules on how you can use your Internet account.

Netiquette

In general, many of the guidelines around *netiquette*, or network etiquette, are simple common sense. But in the rush of being able to communicate with millions of people across thousands of miles, common sense can sometimes get lost along the way. Some examples follow.

:-)When sending e-mail to someone you do not know, be courteous. Imagine how you would behave if you were telephoning a stranger—you would introduce yourself, explain why you wanted to talk to that person, and what you wanted from them. Some people send out e-mail to a number of users at a time, simply asking to talk, but without having a particular subject in mind or a reason for selecting that particular user. The equivalent would be dialing numbers at random out of a telephone book and expecting the person at the other end to be glad for an opportunity to chat.

:-) Similarly, before sending a request to initiate a real-time conversation, ask yourself why you are doing this and how the other person is likely to respond. If they are in the middle of downloading a file, your request will interrupt their transmission. In any case, they will need to stop what they are doing to be able to respond to you. Unless the other person is someone you know, e-mail is almost always more appropriate because the person can respond to it at their convenience. Simply sending out chat requests to everyone, asking them, for instance, why they are logged in at 8 a.m. on Saturday, is not necessarily a good way to make new friends.

:-(When people online get angry at you, they may perform an action known as flaming. *Flaming* generally involves sending e-mail or posting a message expressing their anger in no uncertain terms, often by calling the victim names. The victim may respond similarly, as may friends of either the victim or the flamer. At this point, it becomes known as a *flamefest*. Flames are seldom productive, especially once they reach the flamefest stage.

Do your best not to contribute. Some people deliberately start flames as a way to get attention—for example, posting a message in a group devoted to Star Trek that anybody who watches Star Trek must be an idiot. The best way to deal with such messages is to ignore them. And, of course, never start such discussions yourself. If you do that, angry readers may contact the system administrator at your system, which could result in your losing your account.

~:-/ Remember the readers of your e-mail and Netnews postings have only your words to go by. So make an attempt to make a good impression by spelling your words correctly, using correct grammar, and being clear in your phrasing. The most intelligent people can look like idiots if their language is poor. Also, avoid using all capital letters; aside from looking as though you are shouting, they are more difficult to read (or, as one Internet user says, "It's like watching a herd of rectangular zebras gallop by").

:-| **Like memos, e-mail messages and Netnews postings have** Subject: **lines to tell the reader what they are about.** Use this feature, naming your messages carefully and changing the Subject: line when the one it has is no longer appropriate.

CONTEXT IS THE KEY

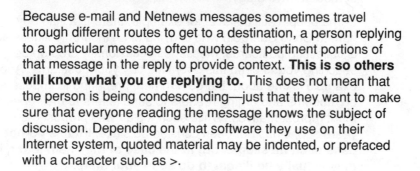

Because e-mail and Netnews messages sometimes travel through different routes to get to a destination, a person replying to a particular message often quotes the pertinent portions of that message in the reply to provide context. **This is so others will know what you are replying to.** This does not mean that the person is being condescending—just that they want to make sure that everyone reading the message knows the subject of discussion. Depending on what software they use on their Internet system, quoted material may be indented, or prefaced with a character such as >.

:-o **Quoted material should be used judiciously.** It is not necessary to quote an entire five-page e-mail message and append "I agree." Leave just enough of the original message to provide context.

;^/ **Before replying to a question, check the rest of the newsgroup or your mailbox to see whether someone else has already answered the question.** There may be some delay between e-mail messages and postings. This becomes a factor when someone asks a question in a Netnews group and gets hundreds of replies. Unless it is a question that you feel you are particularly suited to answer—for example, a question about one of your company's products—consider not answering; no doubt someone else will post the answer, and why contribute to Net clutter?

CHAIN LETTERS AND URBAN LEGENDS

Occasionally, messages start traveling around the network, seemingly of their own accord. Such messages include chain letters ("Send $5 to the first name at the end of this letter, append your own name, and send the letter to eight of your friends.") and some of the more common *urban legends*, a kind of modern mythology.

Some people still believe, for example, there is a little boy named Craig Shergold who is dying of an incurable illness and is collecting postcards. Messages occasionally crop up beseeching you to send this poor little boy your postcards. Another example is one about the government preparing to impose a tax on modems and urging readers to send letters to their government representatives. While such a plan was proposed several years ago, it has not been considered since. **Please do not pass such messages on; in the case of the chain letter, it may actually be illegal to do so in your state.**

{:-] **Learn to communicate your emotions.** It can be difficult to tell whether someone is joking when all your see is their words, with no vocal inflections or body language. Consequently, some people use symbols in their text to indicate their state of mind when writing the message. These symbols are known as *emoticons* or *smileys*. The basic symbol is generally :-). Note that, if you look at it sideways, it looks like a smiling face. Variations include :-(, ;-), and many others. See Appendix D for a plethora of smileys.

l-) **Keep your cool.** In any case, remember that you cannot always tell what a person might be thinking when they write something. Try not to read too much meaning into their message, especially if you think they are angry or making fun of you. If you are not sure, ask them; do not simply assume you have been insulted and leap to your defense.

;-\ **Be selective; don't crowd the network.** When passing on or trying to get information from a variety of people, it is tempting to do so in as many places as possible to maximize your information's or question's exposure. But try to avoid this. Rather than posting your Netnews message to all 20 newsgroups and mailing lists that you think are appropriate, pick one or two of the most appropriate and send the message just to them.

Just the FAQs

In some newsgroups and mailing lists, certain questions are asked so often that these questions and their answers are codified into a file called a *FAQ*, for Frequently Asked Questions. Examples of FAQs include "How do I find an Internet account near me?" or "How do I send e-mail to my friend on CompuServe?"

This file may be posted to the newsgroup or mailing list periodically, or you may be able to download it. Before posting a question that could be common, check to see whether a FAQ file is available, and read through it. The FAQ file may answer many other questions for you.

The Netnews group `news.answers` consists entirely of FAQs.

Unix

More than likely, the computer on which you get your Internet account will be running the Unix operating system. Some people find Unix intimidating because it was designed for programmers and the commands are not necessarily easy to use or remember. Rather than giving users complex commands, Unix gives users many simple commands that can be linked together like building blocks.

But because Unix was designed for programmers, you do not need to know the vast majority of Unix commands. You can get by with the following eight commands for probably 90 percent of what you will need to do.

Remember that Unix is case-sensitive and you should use lowercase letters unless specified. You need to press the Return key (Enter) after each command for it to be executed.

ls—LiSt

The ls command lists the files that you have in your directory on the Internet system, much like the dir command does in DOS.

The ls command also has two modifiers that you may find useful. The first is -l (for Long), and it is appended to the ls command as follows: ls -l (with a space in between). Using -l gives you additional information about each file, such as its size and the date it was last changed.

The second is -a (for All), and it is appended to the ls command as follows: ls -a (with a space in between). Using -a lists files that are not normally shown with the basic ls command—system files that begin with a period (.). You can also use it with the -l command at the same time: **ls -a -l** (or **ls -l -a**; the order of the modifiers does not matter).

An example of ls -a -l output is shown in figure 1.7.

```
Terminal type is vt100
{netcom:1} ls -a -l
total 42
drwx------    3 sharon        512 Jun  8 21:48 .
drwxr-xr-x451 root          7680 Jun  9 10:00 ..
-rw-------    1 sharon        224 Jun  8 14:41 .cshrc
drwx------    2 sharon        512 Jun  8 14:41 .eln
-rw-------    1 sharon        600 Jun  8 14:41 .login
-rw-------    1 sharon        505 Jun  8 14:41 .profile
-rw-------    1 sharon      13610 Jun  8 21:48 RMAIL
-rw-------    1 sharon      13492 Jun  8 21:48 RMAIL~
-rw-------    1 sharon        823 Jun  8 16:00 bounce
{netcom:2}
```

```
ALT-F10  HELP  | ANSI-BBS |  FDX  |  2400 N81 | LOG CLOSED | PRT OFF | CR |  CR
```

Figure 1.7:

Output of the ls command.

rm—ReMove

Sometimes you will want to delete a file. The way to do this is with the rm command—simply type **rm *filename*,** where *filename* is the name of the file that you want to delete.

Note that Unix will not ask you Are you sure? or otherwise check with you—if you tell it to delete the file, it will be gone. So make sure you really want to delete the file, and spell its name carefully, before you press the Return key.

rmdir—ReMove DIRectory

Unix, like DOS, has the ability to use hierarchical file organization in directories. For example, if you are reading Netnews and save a posting that you read, the Internet system you are using will most likely save it in a News directory. But if you have no more need of a directory, you may want to delete it. To do so, type *rmdir directoryname*, where *directoryname* is the name of the directory that you want to delete.

Note that Unix will not delete the directory if there are still files in it; you must remove (rm) all the files in the directory before you can remove (rmdir) the directory.

cat—conCATenate

The cat command is generally used to type the contents of a file onto your screen, as follows: **cat *filename***, where *filename* is the name of the file you want to see.

But if the file is bigger than a few lines, the Unix system may display it on the screen so fast that you miss the top of the file as it scrolls off your screen. In that case, you may want to use the more command.

more—the MORE pager

The more command displays the file in screen-sized chunks and then pauses, waiting for you to press the Return key (Enter) before it displays the next chunk. Like cat, you just type **more *filename***, where *filename* is the name of the file you want to see.

cp—CoPy

Sometimes you want another copy of a file—perhaps because you plan to modify it, and you want to save an original, or perhaps because you want to change a file's name. The cp command works as follows: **cp *existingfilename newfilename***, where ***existingfilename*** is the name of the file that you have now, and ***newfilename*** is the name of the file you want to create.

du -s—Disk Use

In most cases, the Internet system on which you get an account will limit the amount of disk storage you can use in the same way that the hard disk on your PC will only hold a certain amount of information. The du -s command will tell you how much space, in thousands of bytes, that you are using.

man—MANual

Unix documentation is stored on-line, so if you want information about other Unix commands or more detailed information on these commands, you can get the documentation by typing **man *command***, where ***command*** is the Unix command you would like information about.

Unix Special Characters

In addition, Unix uses special characters to perform other functions. Four of the most common are ¦ (pipe), > (redirect output), * (star), and ! (exclamation point or bang).

¦—pipe

This character is the vertical bar, and it takes the output from one Unix command and automatically sends it to another one.

For example, if you call up a list (ls) of your directory, but it is so large that the top scrolls of your screen, you can combine the ls command with the more pager so that Unix displays only one screenful of your directory at a time. You type **ls ¦ more** to do this.

>—redirect output

Like the ¦ character, > sends output from a command somewhere else, but where ¦ sends it to another command, > sends it to a file.

For example, if you want to call up a list (ls) of your directory, but you want to save the information in a file, you can do this by typing **ls > *filename***. Then, instead of appearing on your screen, your directory will appear in filename.

*—star

As in DOS or the Macintosh, * is a *wildcard* character that matches any other character or characters in that position. You can use it to find a file when you are not sure of its whole name, or to find several files that start with the same name.

If you have received several party invitations on e-mail, for example, and you want to be reminded of their dates, you type **ls party***, and Unix will show you any file name that begins with party.

!—exclamation point or bang

Like *, ! is a wildcard character, except that where * can represent any number of characters, ! represents only a single character.

For example, if you type **ls party!**, Unix will show you any file name that begins with party and is followed by a single number or letter, such as partya or party1. But Unix will not show you file names that begin with party and are followed by more than one number or letter, such as party23.

Security

Any time that a computer has the capability to communicate with another computer, its user is taking a risk that someone else, someone unauthorized, might do so as well. Consequently, when you get onto the Internet, you need to protect your Internet account, your files there, and the files on your PC, against intrusion.

An example of unauthorized intrusion occurred in 1988, when a college student named Robert Morris wrote a program that exploited certain flaws in the Unix operating system. The program let him find out passwords, log onto those machines through the Internet, and then find the passwords located on those machines. The program took up so much space on those machines that many of them crashed.

Morris was later caught, and was sentenced to three years' probation, a $10,000 fine, and 400 hours of community service.

An unauthorized user cannot log onto your PC just because you are using the PC to dial up a system on the Internet. Morris' program, for example, ran on only a couple of kinds of Unix systems, and could not run on a PC or Mac. But if you download PC software from a site on the Internet and then use that software, you need to make sure that you have not downloaded a *virus*. In addition, you need to protect the files on your Internet system and your account there.

Protecting Your Internet Account—Choosing a Password

When you get your account on the Internet, you either choose or are assigned a password. In the same way that you have a key to your house, your password is the key to your account. And in the same way that you do not want to leave your keys around, you do not want someone else to get your password.

This means selecting your password carefully and protecting it once you get it.

A well-selected password has the following characteristics:

➡ It is not a word in the English language. In fact, ideally it should not be a word in any language. One of the ways that Robert Morris' program broke into computers was by trying each of the words in the Unix system dictionary as a password.

➡ It should not be your name, your login ID, or the name of your spouse or child. Remember the movie *War Games*? The character played by Matthew Broderick broke into a supposedly secure computer by guessing that the programmer would use the name of his child as a password. Tests on some systems have indicated that as many as one-third of the users set their password to be the same as their login ID!

➡ Your password should include a mix of upper- and lower-case letters, numbers, and special characters to increase the number of possible combinations that a program or an intruder would have to try to guess. In fact, your Internet provider may *require* that you use such a mix.

➡ Some people choose passwords by taking a phrase that is meaningful to them, and using the initials of each word in the phrase. For example, one user who is a professional chef used 1Gis4q as a password—meaning "1 Gallon is 4 quarts."

Once you have chosen your password, guard it carefully. Do not write it down—instead, choose something you can easily remember. Do not give out your password.

YOU SIMPLY CAN'T BE TOO CAREFUL

Some users with accounts on multiple machines choose the same password for all their accounts. This method has advantages and disadvantages. The advantage is you have fewer passwords to remember and keep track of. The disadvantage is that, if an unauthorized user knows that you do this, the person only has to break into one of your accounts to get at them all. If you do choose to make all your passwords the same, do not tell anyone that you have done this.

The other issue is that of changing passwords. Some experienced users recommend that you change your password frequently, and some systems even require it. On the other hand, other users say the frequent changes make keeping track of your current password more difficult, that you will tire of creating new passwords, and thus will get lazy about selecting them.

Certainly, if your Internet provider tells you that there have been attempted break-ins on your system, you should consider changing your password. Also, when you log in, the system will usually tell you when you last logged in. Pay attention to this information, and if it does not match your recollection, change your password and inform your Internet provider.

BEWARE THE BOGUS "AUTHORITY" MESSAGE

Never give your password out in mail messages. One way to break in is to send users a mail message saying you are the system administrator and because of "security" reasons they should send you their passwords. NO ONE has a valid reason to have your password. Never believe requests like this.

On a Unix system, you change your password with the `passwd` command. First, type **passwd** and press the Return (Enter) key. Unix will then ask you to type your old password (to prove that you have the authority to change the password), then the new one, and then will ask you to type the new one again, to make sure you did not mistype it the first time.

DON'T LEAVE INTERNET UNATTENDED

Also, it is unwise to go off and leave your Internet session unattended if there are other people around. It is possible that someone could damage your files or send out insulting e-mail or Netnews postings under your name.

Protecting Your Files On the Internet System

Next, you need to protect your files on the Internet system. If it is running Unix, then when files are created, the Unix system may be set up so that other users on the system can read them, or even modify them, as the default. Moreover, some Unix users feel that a file's owner is responsible for securing it, and that if a file is not secure, then it is permissible for them to read it. Consequently, if you do not want other people to read your files, it is up to you to protect them.

First, you should look at your files to see what protections they have already. You can do this with the `ls -1` command, as shown in figure 1.8.

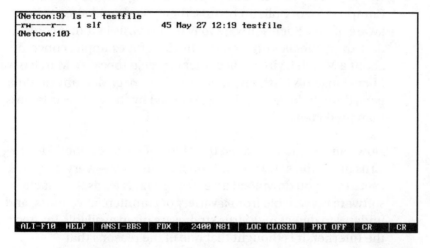

```
{Netcon:9} ls -l testfile
-rw----r--  1 slf          45 May 27 12:19 testfile
{Netcon:10}
```

```
ALT-F10   HELP  | ANSI-BBS | FDX |  2400 N81  | LOG CLOSED | PRT OFF |  CR  |  CR
```

Figure 1.8:

Looking at file permissions with `ls -1`.

For each kind of file, there are three categories of permissions: user, group, and other. What you need to be most concerned about is user and other.

For each of the three categories, there are three types of access to a file: read, write, and execute. Read means a person in that category can read the file; write means a person in that category can make changes to the file; and execute means that a person in that category can run the file, if it is a program.

To change the permissions on a file, use the chmod command, with a plus sign (+) to add a permission and a minus sign (-) to take a permission away. You also specify u or o to set the permission for that category.

For example, `chmod o-rwx` *`filename`* will mean that nobody else will be able to read, write, or execute the file specified by *`filename`*.

Protecting the Files On Your PC or Mac

If you are downloading software from an Internet site to run on your PC, then you need to be concerned about protecting those files as well. If you have been downloading software from CompuServe or bulletin boards, then you should already be aware of this. Such software may have a virus in it that could destroy all the files on your PC. In 1992, for example, concern about a March 6 virus called Michelangelo (because March 6 was Michelangelo's birthday) made the front page of many newspapers, though the actual damage caused by the virus was far less than predicted.

How can you guard against this? First of all, it is a good idea to get virus detection software and run it frequently—every day, plus every time you download a new program, is advisable. Such software is available from a variety of commercial vendors, and updates to detect new virus strains are often available for free on the Internet. It is thought that one of the reasons that Michelangelo was not as devastating as some had warned was because all the concern inspired users to run virus software to remove Michelangelo before March 6.

In addition, some software repositories require that any software must be deposited in its original, source code form, so that people can examine it for viruses.

Finally, you should back up your data often. Many corporations do a full backup of all the data every week, and do an incremental backup of just the changed data every day. If you do frequent backups, then you can restore your data if you lose it—whether to a virus or to a hard disk crash.

Summary

At this point, you should now have the information necessary to find yourself an Internet account, set it up, know basic guidelines for behavior, and protect your files. You can now begin to use the Internet to meet people and get information.

CHAPTER 2

Connecting with Other Individuals

E-mail or electronic mail is the term used to refer to any messages sent from one user to another. You also might receive
e-mail messages generated by the computer's system you are
using. So far, e-mail is even more fun to receive than paper mail
from the U.S. Postal Service ("snail mail" in Internet lingo). The
reason is that although you can get some junk e-mail, most bills
still come on paper.

After you begin to use e-mail, you might wonder how you ever
lived without it. You can write messages to people any time you
want, and don't have to worry about waking them up with the
telephone; penmanship, paper, and stamps aren't a bother. It's
simply much easier to stay in touch with e-mail. This chapter
tells you:

➡ How to write, address, mail, and reply to e-mail, including
   e-mail on other on-line services

➡ How to find mailing lists, subscribe to them, and
   unsubscribe to them

➡ How to handle e-mail problems

➡ How to communicate in real-time with individuals or groups

➡ How to find MUDs and MUSEs, and how to use them

What Is E-Mail?

Riding the Internet highway grants you access to one of the fastest, most efficient and convenient mail systems ever invented. You already know that when you have an Internet connection, your computer is connected to an enormous number of other computers. You, the user, also have a connection to all the other users of Internet. In this chapter you will learn how to use the Internet e-mail system.

You can send e-mail to a hundred people as easily as to one. You can include copies of pertinent text from another person in your letter, rather than reminding them of what he or she said. And e-mail offers instant gratification; the message arrives in seconds or minutes, while your mood and words are fresh.

E-mail is not the only way to communicate with individuals on the computer. You can use mailing lists, which automatically send messages to everyone on the list—a sort of private discussion group. You can use real-time chat, which enables you to communicate with one or more people at the same time, thousands of miles away. (Imagine a high-tech CB radio.)

Then you have multiuser dungeons (MUDs) and multiuser simulation environments (MUSEs), which fall into a category of their own. Technically, MUDs and MUSEs are games, but for some Internet users, they virtually become a separate world.

What Your E-Mail Address Is

Remember when you were little and you had to learn your own address before you could go out on your own? Well, the Internet is no different—it is a good idea to know where you are and the way to reach you.

SAME PLACE, DIFFERENT ADDRESS?

Technically, several different kinds of e-mail addresses can be used on the Internet, and it is not always easy to tell which kind. For example, just because an address has an @ does not mean it's an Internet address. However, such distinctions are becoming less important to the average user as the links between networks become more transparent, so this book occasionally refers to e-mail addresses as "Internet addresses," even though they might be, for example, UUCP addresses. No generic term exists now for "e-mail addresses for the Internet and all systems connected to the Internet," and even Internet mavens argue about what such addresses should be called.

Finding Your Address and What It Means

The important thing for you to do is to learn your address. You can always learn this from your Internet provider. Like a regular Post Office address, an Internet address has a *name*—the login ID—as well as an address, generally separated by an @. You can break the address down to the computer's name followed by information about the computer's domain. A *domain* is a group the computer belongs to. Examples of domains include geographic ones (such as sf.ca.us., to signify San Francisco, California, United States), or organizational ones, such as are shown in table 2.1.

Domain Name	Meaning
.com	Commercial
.edu	Educational institution
.gov	Government body
.mil	Military
.org	Organization (any group that doesn't fall under the other types)

Table 2.1

Organizational Domains

Other indicators that appear in addresses include `.uucp` or `.bitnet`, each of which indicates that the computer system at least historically was attached through one of these other networks.

DOMAINS: NOT ALWAYS WHAT THEY SEEM

Geographical domains are guidelines and do not necessarily represent the actual physical location of the machine. For example, one computer in the `sf.ca.us` domain is actually in Cambridge, Massachusetts. It was originally in the San Francisco Bay Area, but the owner moved, and changing the address tables associated with the machine was harder than keeping the existing name.

For example, here are two different types of address:

```
slf@netcom.com

slf@well.sf.ca.us
```

The first address is of a machine registered through the organization domain, and the second through the geographic domain. The interesting thing about this example is that both machines are public-access Unix systems in the San Francisco Bay Area. But one organization chose one style and the other organization chose the other style. This demonstrates that Internet addresses can be ordered according to either geographical location or the type of institution. This is unlike post office addresses, which are always geographical.

Non-U.S. countries almost always use the geographic domain, with a two-character country code at the end of the address (like the `.us` in the preceding example). For example, `.uk` stands for the United Kingdom. A complete list of country codes is given in the Internet Country Codes, Appendix C.

Dissecting the Address

How does an e-mail message addressed to slf@netcom.com actually get there? The company that set up the Netcom computers went to the Internet Network Information Center (NIC) and registered their machines. Every machine that Netcom owns has a numeric address of four numbers, separated by periods, called an *Internet Protocol*, or IP, number. The NIC grants Netcom the IP numbers and associates the name netcom.com (plus netcom2, netcom3, and so on, for each individual machine) with those numbers.

Just like Netcom, all computer addresses on Internet also have a numeric location composed of four numbers separated by dots or periods. Each number can be one, two, or three digits. For example, there is a machine at Indiana University locally known as "aqua." The full Internet address is aqua@ucs.indiana.edu. The IP number of this same machine is 129.79.1.2. The number 129 is the domain—in this case, all of Indiana University; 79 is the subdomain, the Bloomington campus; 1 is the subnet; and 2 is the node on the subnet 1. This corresponds to elements in the address aqua@ucs.indiana.edu. The first part, aqua, is the node, which might be a machine name or a user name, ucs is the subdomain, and indiana is the domain.

The address of an account on aqua might be something like 129.79.71.2.1022. Now, remember that IP numbers are for machines or nodes and have only four parts. The 1022 of the account address is a user number and not part of the IP address.

Each machine on the Internet learns about the other machines through the Domain Name Server (DNS) database. Every time two machines on the Internet communicate, they exchange information about the other machines each one knows.

When you send e-mail to another machine, the mail system looks up the machine's name in the DNS and retrieves the address. The e-mail is sent to the mail port—the machine that accepts incoming mail—on that address; the route the e-mail takes is determined by routers. *Routers* are hardware devices that figure out the most efficient path for data to take.

Just to keep things confusing, there is another way Internet mail might be addressed, called *domain name addressing*. Domain name addressing began to be used commonly just a few years ago. The capability to send a message simply to

name@machinename.organization

has made the Internet much easier to use. Be careful with this, though; it won't work for all addresses.

ADDRESSES WITH A BANG

You occasionally might see addresses containing an !, called a *bang*, or a %. These symbols can mean that the user with this kind of address is not directly connected to the Internet, but does have partial access and can send and receive mail. Remember, you don't have to understand how the address works to use it.

If you receive e-mail from somebody, the message can include a long string of computer names at the beginning of the message, or *header*, through which the message goes to get from the sender to you. More than likely, though, you don't need to worry about this; the e-mail probably includes the much simpler version:

username@machinename.organization

This is a return address, in the header or at the end of the message. In particular, some major companies, such as Sun Microsystems Inc., are set up so that, although each person might have an individual e-mail address on that company's network—such as the following:

username@machinename.division.sun.com

you can send e-mail to the person simply by using this next address:

username@sun.com

This leads to a good example of domain addressing. At Indiana University, all mail comes through a machine called "iugate," which is smart enough to sort out all local addresses. Therefore, `seeker@indiana.ed` works just as well as `seeker@aqua.ucs.indiana.edu`.

Basic E-Mail Commands

For simplicity, this chapter uses `mail`, the basic Unix e-mail package, which is widely available and easy to use. If you have an Internet connection, you probably also have access to this program. You access it while logged into your Internet account. The next section discusses other e-mail software options available on your Internet system provider.

Reading Your Mail

When you log in to your Internet provider, you might be greeted by one of the following messages:

```
You have new mail.
```

or

```
You have mail.
```

This depends on the way your Internet system is set up. Some systems differentiate between mail you had but had not read when you last logged off and mail that has entered an empty mailbox; some do not.

In addition, if more e-mail arrives as you work, your Internet system might tell you:

```
You have more mail.
```

In any case, to read e-mail sent to you, type **mail** and press Enter. At that point, `mail` displays something like figure 2.1.

```
Terminal type is vt100
{netcom2:1} mail
Mail version SMI 4.0 Thu Jul 23 13:52:20 PDT 1992  Type ? for help.
"/usr/spool/mail/sharon": 3 messages 3 new
>N  1 support              Tue Jun  8 14:41   99/4390  Welcome
 N  2 slf                  Tue Jun  8 15:36   12/349   party
 N  3 slf                  Tue Jun  8 15:37   78/2822  [rob@agate.berkeley.edu:
&
```

```
ALT-F10  HELP | ANSI-BBS | FDX |  2400 N81 | LOG CLOSED | PRT OFF | CR |   CR
```

Figure 2.1:

Incoming mail.

To read a particular message, type the number of the message
and press Enter, or just press Enter, and the next e-mail message
appears (see fig. 2.2).

```
Message  5:
From hchan@cns.nyu.edu Tue Jun  8 17:07:03 1993
Return-Path: <hchan@cns.nyu.edu>
Received: from [192.76.177.18] by mail.netcom.com (5.65/SMI-4.1/Netcom)
        id AA02911; Tue, 8 Jun 93 17:07:01 -0700
Received: from WOTAN.CNS.NYU.EDU by cmcl2.NYU.EDU (5.61/1.34)
        id AA18756; Tue, 8 Jun 93 20:08:49 -0400
Received: by wotan.cns.nyu.edu (4.1/SMI-4.0)
        id AA18098; Tue, 8 Jun 93 20:09:00 EDT
Date: Tue, 8 Jun 93 20:09:00 EDT
From: hchan@cns.nyu.edu (Hoover Chan)
Message-Id: <9306090009.AA18098@wotan.cns.nyu.edu>
To: sharon@netcom.com
Subject: Greetings from New York City!
Status: R

Hi, Sharon. Here's some e-mail from the Big Apple (actually, the
Center for Neural Sciences at New York University in Washington
Square).

- Hoover

&
```

```
ALT-F10  HELP | ANSI-BBS | FDX |  2400 N81 | LOG CLOSED | PRT OFF | CR |   CR
```

Figure 2.2:

An e-mail message.

Saving Your Mail

After you read the message, what do you do with it? Perhaps you
want to save it. To save the message, type **s** *filename* and press
Enter, where *filename* is the name of the file to which the message
is stored. If *filename* already exists, the message is *appended*, or

attached, to the end of the existing file, and the other data in the file does not change.

Deleting Your Mail

Maybe you don't need the message after you read it. Just type **d** and press Enter. That deletes the message.

You also can delete a message from the prompt in the `mail` system. If you don't want to read message 3, or if you read message 3 and later decide to delete it, type **d3** and press Enter. Further, you can delete many messages with one command; d345 deletes messages 3 through 5, for example.

BUGS ON THE `mail` WINDSHIELD

Many versions of the `mail` program have a *bug*, or program error, connected to deleting a message. If you delete a message by typing d and pressing Enter, and then press Enter again to read the next message, you don't see the next message, but the one after that. In other words, if you just read and delete message 3 and then press Enter, you get message 5, not message 4. Message 4 is not gone, but you have to read it explicitly by typing 4 and pressing Enter.

Undeleting Your Message

If you delete a message, but are still in `mail` and decide to keep it after all, type **u**, for undelete, then the message number, and press Enter. The message is then back in your mailbox. For example, to undelete the third message, if you deleted it, type u3.

Remember that after you exit `mail`, deleted messages remain deleted. You cannot return to `mail` and type u to recover a message.

Replying to Your Message

Maybe you want to reply to the message—for example, RSVP to an invitation. Type **r** and press Enter. Note that `mail` will automatically address the e-mail message for you, including a subject header.

HOW TO GET RETURN ADDRESS RIGHT

Sometimes the return address calculated by `mail` is not the most efficient. It might consist of a string of addresses rather than the simple *username@machinename.organization*. Or the return address might be completely wrong. If you can't send a message using Reply, you need to send the e-mail manually. See the section "Sending E-mail" later in this chapter.

Then, type your message.

The `mail` editor in your system may or may not have *word wrap*. If it doesn't, you have to press Enter at the end of each line, like on an old typewriter; if it does, the editor wraps text to the next line automatically.

After you type your message, type **.** as the first and only character on a line and press Enter to send it to the recipient.

Oops! Aborting a Reply

If you begin to reply to a message, but change your mind, type ^**c** (c while holding down the Ctrl key). When you do this, `mail` replies `Interrupt -- one more to kill letter`. So type ^**c** again to confirm that you really do want to abort the message.

Replying to a Message Sent to Multiple Persons

If you get a message that has been sent to several people and you want to reply to it, you have two options: reply to the person who sent the message or reply to everyone on the list. Most of the time, type r to reply to everyone, or type R to reply to just the sender.

FOR REPLIES, CHECK THE MESSAGE HEADER!

This is not universal! Some systems on the Internet are set up so that you type R to reply to everyone and r to reply to only to the sender. You can see which is the case in your system by checking the message header: Is the message addressed to multiple people, or just one? If you choose incorrectly, abort the message by typing ^c twice, as explained earlier.

Checking Mail Headers

Several lines of information appear at the top of every mail message. Some of this information you might find useful, and most of it you will learn to ignore (see fig. 2.3).

```
         id AA02911; Tue, 8 Jun 93 17:07:01 -0700
Received: from WOTAN.CNS.NYU.EDU by cncl2.NYU.EDU (5.61/1.34)
         id AA18756; Tue, 8 Jun 93 20:08:49 -0400
Received: by wotan.cns.nyu.edu (4.1/SMI-4.0)
         id AA18098; Tue, 8 Jun 93 20:09:00 EDT
Date: Tue, 8 Jun 93 20:09:00 EDT
From: hchan@cns.nyu.edu (Hoover Chan)
Message-Id: <9306090009.AA18098@wotan.cns.nyu.edu>
To: sharon@netcom.com
Subject: Greetings from New York City!
Status: R

Hi, Sharon. Here's some e-mail from the Big Apple (actually, the
Center for Neural Sciences at New York University in Washington
Square).

- Hoover


& r
To: hchan@cns.nyu.edu
Subject: Re:  Greetings from New York City!

ALT-F10  HELP │ ANSI-BBS │ FDX │ 2400 N81 │ LOG CLOSED │ PRT OFF │ CR  │  CR
```

Figure 2.3:

Typical information that appears with mail messages.

The two most informative lines are the From and Subject lines. A command in mail shows you just this information for each of the letters in your mail box.

If you receive a number of e-mail messages, and read some of them and delete others, you can lose track of what is in your mailbox. To see what you still have, type h and press Enter. As a result, mail responds in a fashion akin to figure 2.4.

Exiting Mail

You can leave the mail program in several ways. Typically, you quit the program (that is, type q and press Enter).

```
550 listserv@sunyside.sunnyside.com... Host unknown

     ----- Unsent message follows -----
Return-Path: <sharon>
Received: by netcom.netcom.com (5.65/SMI-4.1/Netcom)
        id AA02614; Tue, 8 Jun 93 18:44:50 -0700
Date: Tue, 8 Jun 93 18:44:50 -0700
From: sharon (Sharon Fisher)
Message-Id: <9306090144.AA02614@netcom.netcom.com>
To: listserv@sunyside.sunnyside.com
Subject: join bawit

join bawit

& d
& h
 U  1 slf             Tue Jun  8 15:36    13/359   party
 U  2 slf             Tue Jun  8 15:37    79/2832  [rob@agate.berkeley.edu:
 N  3 Mailer-Daemon   Tue Jun  8 15:58    26/813   Returned mail: User unkno
 N  4 gail@well.sf.ca.us Tue Jun  8 16:16  35/1135  Re:  bawit
 N  6 friday          Tue Jun  8 18:04    16/472   Talk
>N  8 listserv@sunyside.com Tue Jun  8 18:44   28/1087  Error Condition Re: Inv
al
&
 ALT-F10  HELP  │ ANSI-BBS │ FDX │ 2400 N81 │ LOG CLOSED │ PRT OFF │ CR │  CR
```

Figure 2.4:

Checking mail headers.

If you choose to quit, all the messages you delete are gone for good. Also, if you read a message, but neither delete nor save it in a file elsewhere, mail displays a message similar to the following:

    3 messages saved in mbox.

What this means is that mail automatically creates a file called mbox, and all the messages are stored in it. You tell mail you want to read these messages by typing **mail -f mbox** and pressing Enter. This gives you the saved messages in mbox and all your new messages.

DELETING THE mbox FILE

If you are not diligent about deleting your e-mail as you read it, your mbox file can get very large without your noticing it. But your system administrator does, and by then, clearing it out can be quite a job, just like if the in-box on your desk overflows if you don't file anything. You can delete the entire mbox file by using the Unix rm command. Type **rm mbox** and press Enter. If mail needs to save messages in an mbox again, it creates a new one.

It also is possible to use the `-f` option to view files of mail messages you have saved. Remember, if you save a mail message to a file that already exists, it will be appended to the end of that file. After you save several mail messages to the same file, you might be paging for a long time through that file to find the information you are looking for. If you use the command mail `-f saved_messages_file`, that file will look like another mail box, and you can access the individual letters again.

Sending E-Mail

To send e-mail to someone, type **mail** followed by their user name and address, then press Enter. To send mail to multiple people, just separate each one by a comma.

```
mail slf@netcom.com,slf@well.sf.ca.us
```

The `mail` command then gives you a `Subject:` field, into which you type the subject of your message. It helps your recipients if you choose a meaningful `Subject:`.

Otherwise, sending a message is much like replying to one. Type your message. As when you reply to a message, the mail program at your site may or may not have *word wrap*. Try it on your machine and see.

As with replying to a message, you can abort the e-mail message by typing **^c** twice.

When you are ready to send the message, type **.** in the first column as the only character in that line and press Enter.

Sending Files through the Mail

Sometimes you will find it easier to compose your message with your own editor and then send the completed letter through e-mail. It is possible to send a text file to another user.

The `mail` command works in at least three different ways. So far you have have learned what happens when you type the `mail` command like this:

```
mail
```

Remember, you use the command this way to read and reply to your mail messages. You also used the command this way:

```
mail user@address
```

This is the command you just used to send a mail message.

To send an ASCII file through the e-mail system, all you have to do is direct the file to the `mail` command:

```
mail seeker@address < my_file
```

The command to send a file is just a logical extension of the `mail` command. You first type **mail**, and then the user and address you want to send the file to. Then use the < (less than) to direct the file you want to send into the command sending it. Don't let the < symbol confuse you and you won't have any trouble.

Using Tilde Commands

So far you have seen many of the commands that can be used within the mail system. Each of these commands is a single letter and can be used only at the mail prompt. Commands that are used while you are in the middle of typing an e-mail message are called *tilde commands*. "Tilde" is the name of the character ~, which should appear to the left of the number one on your keyboard. The tilde enables you to send a command to the mail system; any letter typed after the tilde is not a part of the letter, but is considered a command. As you might guess, each of the tilde commands begins with a ~.

Suppose you want to include an existing file in your e-mail message. You can do this by typing **~r filename**, where *filename* is the name of the file to include.

Another useful tilde command is ~p, which will show you what you have written so far. This is helpful if your letter is long and scrolling off the screen.

Sometimes you will make mistakes while composing an e-mail message. You can drop into your editor with the ~v command. Just use the editor the way you would when writing any file. When you exit the editor you will return to mail where you left it.

This book doesn't devote a lot of space to the tilde commands, but you should at least know that they exist. Without them, e-mail would be much less convenient. You can learn to use them after you feel comfortable with the rest of the mail commands mentioned in this chapter. To see the entire list of tilde commands, type ~?. Remember, the tilde commands work only while you are writing a message, so mail yourself a letter or two and do some experimenting.

ENCODING AND DECODING BINARY FILES

Don't try to send binary files (programs, for example) through e-mail. This does not work. You first must *encode* the file you want to send, and then your recipient must *decode* it. To do this, on a Unix system, type:

```
uuencode binaryfilename > decodedfilename
```

The recipient decodes the file with:

```
uudecode decodedfilename > binaryfilename
```

There is more to the `mail` command than this chapter can cover. The commands in the earlier sections were chosen as the most useful, but there are many others. Bear in mind that you can get more information by using the `man` command. Combine this command with **mail**:

```
man mail
```

This man file is quite large and can tell you more than you ever want to know, but it is the place to look when you are ready to learn more.

Other Kinds of Mail Software

Depending on your Internet provider, you might have several more options for e-mail systems. Some of these are described in the following sections. To see if your Internet provider has them, ask, or try typing the following:

```
man e-mailprogram
```

where e-mailprogram is the name of the e-mail program that you want to check for. Remember that man is the Unix command for manual; if the program is present on the Internet system, man gives you basic instructions to run the program.

emacs

The "thing" known as emacs, or editor for Project MAC at Massachusetts Institute of Technology, is a world unto itself. Technically, it is an *editor*: a piece of software intended to help you create and modify text. But it includes many other features, like a mail program, news reader, and even an implementation of the Tower of Hanoi game.

A detailed description of emacs is beyond the scope of this book—indeed, an entire book could be written just about emacs—but in terms of e-mail, its advantages over standard Unix mail is that it is a full-screen program, rather than line-oriented. It includes the emacs editor features and it enables you to *forward* (send to another user) messages, as well as include copies of the message to which you reply.

The disadvantages of emacs are that it is very large, and cryptic enough to make Unix seem user-friendly. Like Unix itself, it is intended to be powerful, not necessarily easy.

elm

`elm` is another full-screen e-mail program, except that, unlike `emacs`, it is intended to be easy to use. It was written by Dave Taylor and is available on a number of public access Internet systems. It includes a tutorial and extensive documentation, so if your Internet access system has `elm`, you might want to check it out.

pine

`elm`, `pine`—get it? Though `pine` is also a full-screen e-mail program, the difference between it and `elm` is that `pine` is intended for novices and is easy to use.

Another advantage of `pine` is that it supports a new standard, *Multipart Internet Mail Extensions (MIME)*. This standard defines a way for you to attach multimedia e-mail, such as graphics and sounds, to e-mail messages. Although you might not need this feature right now, keep it in mind for the future.

The best way to learn `pine` is through the help screens in the program.

Points to Watch For

E-mail can be very easy and convenient. Sometimes too easy. Before you send off a message written in anger, or that might contain something insulting or bigoted, think about it. Would you say this to the person's face? How do you think he or she would react? Are you perhaps jumping to conclusions? Could he or she take your message the wrong way? Remember, the reader will not see your facial expression to lighten the tone. Because the reader won't see a face or hear a voice, sarcasm and teasing can be interpreted as an attack.

Make sure that your message is addressed correctly—especially if you are replying to a list and intend to send the message only to the sender, not to the whole list. More than once, people have sent large amounts of personal information, intended only for one person, to an entire mailing list. If nothing else, a long series of people RSVPing to an invitation to a party, for example, is wearing for the other people on the list.

It is not polite to pass personal e-mail from one person to another, or to post it to a Netnews group, without asking the sender. Treat others' mail as you would paper mail, but act as though the mail you send is not. After all, this is an imperfect world.

Don't rely on the privacy of e-mail. If you send a message to one person complaining about another, don't be surprised if the subject of your complaints finds out. (You would be surprised how often someone accidentally types in the subject's name as one of the people to receive the e-mail.)

In addition, if your e-mail fails to reach its destination (*bounces*), it can end up being sent to an e-mail postmaster along the way. If you address it incorrectly, it can go to another person with the same login ID at another machine.

Mailing Lists

A mailing list is like a private discussion group, held in e-mail. Unlike Netnews groups, mailing lists have a fairly steady membership, because you must subscribe to them to get the messages. Consequently, they tend to be more focused than many Netnews groups. On the other hand, they can also have much less traffic. Days can go by between postings on a slow mailing list. (But when you begin to subscribe to several mailing lists, you can end up grateful for that.) Others can produce as many as a hundred messages a day.

Some mailing lists are *reflectors*, meaning that a person sends a message to a particular address and the message is automatically sent out to everyone on the list. Others are *digests*, meaning that one person collects the submissions into a single message, and sends it out every few days.

DETOUR SHORTCUT

Some mailing lists are *moderated*, meaning that one person checks over submissions to make sure that they are correct and appropriate for the list before mailing them out.

Some mailing lists are available as Netnews groups and mailing lists, and you can choose which method is more convenient for you. If you receive them as e-mail, for example, they stay in your mailbox until you delete them; this can be an advantage or a disadvantage. On the other hand, if you receive them as Netnews, you can use Netnews features, such as `deleting, unread, all of the messages in an entire conversation`. Netnews groups that contain the word `listserv`, or begin with the word `info`, are also available as mailing lists. (Whether these mailing lists are available as Netnews groups *for you* is something you need to check for your particular system.)

Some people who run mailing lists also have files of interest to mailing list members that they store on their systems, and members can retrieve these files—such as lyrics to all of a particular singer's songs, or back issues of submissions to the mailing list.

Members of a mailing list even have parties and other get-togethers.

Some mailing lists are set up with an automatic program through which you *subscribe* and *unsubscribe* to the list. For others, you send e-mail to the moderator and ask to be added or deleted, and the moderator processes your requests every few days.

Finding Mailing Lists

No single list of all mailing lists exists, but you can find out about them from the following places:

➡ **Netnews groups of the specific interest.** For example, if you read `rec.music.misc`, you periodically see postings about new and existing mailing lists to cover the music of a particular artist. A compilation of musical mailing lists also is posted to the newsgroup occasionally.

➡ **Netnews groups specifically set up to discuss mailing lists.** These often include notifications of new mailing lists.

➡ **Related mailing lists.** People on mailing lists often know of other mailing lists on related topics. They tell you about them if you ask, or they can simply come up in conversation.

➡ **Downloading lists.** Some anonymous FTP sites, such as `ftp.nisc.sri.com`, have lists of mailing lists that you can download. See Chapter 4.

➡ **Request them by e-mail.** Some mailing list programs are automatically set up to send you information about mailing lists if you ask. For example, you can type `mail listserv@bitnic.bitnet` and press Enter, and include the command `list global` in the body of the message. The `listserv` program at that machine automatically e-mails you a large file of mailing lists.

Subscribing to a Mailing List

If you see a mailing list you would like to subscribe to, read the description carefully. Most mailing lists have separate addresses to distinguish between submissions to the list and administrative requests, so members of the list are not burdened with an endless stream of `subscribe` messages.

The convention is that the administrative address is the same as the mailing list address, with `-request` added. In other words, if the mailing list address is as follows:

mailinglist@machinename.organization

the administrative address is as follows:

mailinglist-request@machinename.organization

Also check the description for indications of whether the subscription process is automatic, and if it is, carefully note the command you use to subscribe to the list.

AUTOMATED MAILING LISTS

If the address contains the word `listserv`, the program is more than likely automated. In most such programs, the convention for subscribing to the mailing list is to type the following:

> `mail listserv@`*`machinename.organization`*

You then press Enter, including the following as the body of the message:

> `subscribe` *`mailinglistname Your Name`*

Other mailing list programs use `join` rather than `subscribe`, or ask you to make the subscription request in the subject line of the message rather than in the body.

Automated programs generally send a piece of e-mail back to you telling you if your request to be added to the list was successful (see figs. 2.5 and 2.6).

```
Date: Tue, 8 Jun 1993 18:45:56 -0700
Message-Id: <199306090145.AA09848@snyside.sunnyside.com>
Errors-To: listserv-owner@sunnyside.com
Reply-To: listserv@sunnyside.com
Sender: listserv@sunnyside.com
From: listserv@sunnyside.com
To: sharon@netcom.com
Cc: listserv-owner@sunnyside.com
Subject: Error Condition Re: Invalid request
X-Listserver-Version: 6.0 -- UNIX ListServer by Anastasios Kotsikonas
X-Comment: The CPSR Internet Library
Status: R

>join bawit

Unrecognized request JOIN

Report any problems to 'listserv-owner@sunnyside.com'.
For a list of the available requests send a message to listserv@sunnyside.com
with a body consisting of nothing but the word HELP

PS: Any subsequent requests that you might have submitted have been ignored.

&
ALT-F10  HELP  | ANSI-BBS | FDX  | 2400 N81 | LOG CLOSED | PRT OFF | CR  |  CR
```

Figure 2.5:

An unsuccessful mailing list request.

```
& 9
Message  9:
From listserv@snyside.sunnyside.com Tue Jun  8 18:52:50 1993
Return-Path: <listserv@snyside.sunnyside.com>
Received: from snyside.sunnyside.com by mail.netcom.com (5.65/SMI-4.1/Netcom)
        id AA10412; Tue, 8 Jun 93 18:52:45 -0700
Received: by snyside.sunnyside.com id AA09890
    (5.65c8/IDA-1.4.4 for sharon@netcom.com); Tue, 8 Jun 1993 18:54:34 -0700
Date: Tue, 8 Jun 1993 18:54:34 -0700
Message-Id: <199306090154.AA09890@snyside.sunnyside.com>
Errors-To: bawit-owner@sunnyside.com
Reply-To: listserv@sunnyside.com
Sender: listserv@sunnyside.com
From: listserv@sunnyside.com
To: sharon@netcom.com
Subject: SUBSCRIBE BAWIT-ANNOUNCE SHARON FISHER
X-Listserver-Version: 6.0 -- UNIX ListServer by Anastasios Kotsikonas
X-Comment: The CPSR Internet Library
Status: R

Subscription requests are not automatic for this list. Your request has
been forwarded to bawit-owner@sunnyside.com for approval.

&
ALT-F10  HELP │ ANSI-BBS │ FDX │ 2400 N81 │ LOG CLOSED │ PRT OFF │ CR │   CR
```

Figure 2.6:

A successful
mailing list request.

If your mailing list request fails, check the message the program
sends you for clues. Perhaps you typed the mailing list name
incorrectly, or did not include your name.

Many times, whether the subscription program is automatic, you
get a welcome message from the e-mail administrator, giving you
the rules of the list and other information. Read this through, but
also save it as a file for reference. This message usually also tells
you how to *resign*, or unsubscribe, from the mailing list. Like
cancelling a subscription to a magazine, such requests can take
several days to process.

DON'T FRUSTRATE YOURSELF OR OTHERS

The importance on a social basis of subscribing and
unsubscribing to mailing lists correctly cannot be overempha-
sized. It is terribly annoying for members of the mailing list to
receive dozens of such messages. Similarly, if you are trying to
resign from a list, it is frustrating to continue receiving messages
because you didn't unsubscribe correctly. Also, sending e-mail
to the entire list complaining about the amount of trouble you
are having resigning from the list is never appreciated, or useful.

Mailing to and from Other Systems

Maybe you want to send e-mail to a user on a different on-line service. Fortunately, more and more of these other services are gaining such links.

Table 2.2 shows the way to address an e-mail message to a number of other popular services.

Service	Address Format
America on-line	`AOLid@aol.com`
AppleLink	`AppleLinkID@applelink.apple.com`
AT&T Mail	`ATTMailID%attmail@att.com`
BIX	`BIXid@bix.com`
CompuServe	`xxxxx.xxxx@compuserve.com`, where `xxxxx.xxxx` is the person's usual CompuServe ID, but with a . rather than a ,.
FidoNet	`FidoNetID@fidonetaddress.fidonet.org`
GEnie	`GenieID@genie.geis.com`
MCI Mail	`accountname@mcimail.com` or `FirstName_LastName@mcimail.com` or `MCIMailID@mcimail.com` (using the person's seven-digit MCI Mail number).
SprintMail	`SprintAlias@sprint.com`

Table 2.2

Addressing E-Mail to Other Services

This list is just a guide. You still will need to know a person's user name on each system to send him or her mail. Several telephone book look-up services are under development, but the easiest way to get a person's e-mail address still is to call them up and ask.

How To Deal with E-Mail Problems

Unfortunately, e-mail is imperfect, and subject to the vagaries of the network—not to mention the vagaries of the people using it. If a piece of e-mail does not successfully reach its destination, you often find out from a message in your mailbox like the one in figure 2.7.

```
Date: Tue, 8 Jun 93 15:57:08 -0700
From: Mailer-Daemon (Mail Delivery Subsystem)
Subject: Returned mail: User unknown
Message-Id: <9306082257.AA10057@netcom2.netcom.com>
To: sharon
Status: R

     ----- Transcript of session follows -----
550 n... User unknown

     ----- Unsent message follows -----
Return-Path: <sharon>
Received: by netcom2.netcom.com (5.65/SMI-4.1/Netcom)
        id AA09947; Tue, 8 Jun 93 15:57:08 -0700
Date: Tue, 8 Jun 93 15:57:08 -0700
From: sharon (Sharon Fisher)
Message-Id: <9306082257.AA09947@netcom2.netcom.com>
To: n
Subject: Wondering

I was just wondering what would happen if I sent an email message to someone
whom I know didn't exit.

&
ALT-F10  HELP  | ANSI-BBS | FDX  |  2400 N81  | LOG OPEN  | PRT OFF | CR  |  CR
```

Figure 2.7:

A bounce message.

Although the amount of information in a bounce message can be daunting, looking at it can provide some indication of the problem.

Mistakes Do Happen

Some of the most common types of e-mail errors are *operator errors*, or *pilot errors*, fancy names for saying you made a mistake. For example, a bounce message might include the following phrase:

```
Unknown host
```

This means that the Internet system from which you sent the e-mail does not recognize the name of the Internet system of the e-mail recipient.

First, try checking the address. Are you sure it is correct? Are you sure you typed it correctly? It is easy to mistake - for ., for example, and such a small change does make a difference.

Be especially sure to check the original address if you are replying to a message from the person's e-mail instead of typing in the address yourself; the return addresses created by e-mail `reply` commands are not always accurate.

Similarly, a bounce message might include the following phrase:

```
Unknown user
```

This means that the e-mail reached the other Internet system successfully, but that it did not recognize the `username`. Again, check your transcription and spelling.

FIXING A BOUNCED MESSAGE

If your e-mail message bounces, and you discover that it bounced because you made a typographical error in the address, you do not need to type the entire message over again. Instead, save it as a file, and include it in a new e-mail message. Or, if you are using an e-mail system that supports a `forward` function, forward the message to the correct user name and address. However, it is courteous to remove the many lines of headers and so on contained in the bounce message.

Temporary Delays

Sometimes the bounce message says something like the following:

```
Your message is not deliverable. Delivery will be
attempted for the next three days.
```

Some machines are not always connected to the Internet, but call in periodically to receive their messages. If you receive this message, that could be what is happening. Wait for a few days to see if the message goes through. If it does not, you most likely get another message. Here, you need to send the message again, or find another way to reach the person.

If at First You Don't Succeed...

Sometimes a message bounces—or simply vanishes—because a portion of the Internet goes down or gets overloaded. This is especially likely to occur over a holiday. Then the easiest way to deal with the problem is to try to send your message again. Once.

If you get the same bounce message again, you have what is known as a *repeatable problem*. Your message still did not go through, but at least the Internet is being consistent about it, if that is any consolation.

Repeatable E-Mail Problems

If you are sure you have the correct user name and e-mail address and you still get a bounce, you might need to ask for help. The easiest way to get e-mail information about another system is to send e-mail to the postmaster on that system, as follows:

```
mail postmaster@machine.organization
```

You then explain your problem.

If you are not sure that you have the correct user name and e-mail address, or you cannot e-mail the postmaster because you do not know the name of the machine, the easiest way to check is to contact the person through another method, such as telephoning or asking them. Although this is not as high-tech, it is far simpler and more reliable than any other method.

If telephoning or asking the person is not an option, you might need to use software tools to find the person or their address. See Chapter 5.

Communicating in Real Time

If two people are on-line at the same time, and they might want to have a short discussion, the most convenient way for them to communicate is through a real-time chat facility such as `talk`.

Internet Relay Chat (IRC) is an entire service set up specifically for people on the Internet to communicate with each other in real time, like a CB radio or CompuServe's CB Simulator. It is especially useful for meeting people in other countries who are interested in meeting new people. In addition, some topics are frequently discussed on IRC, and people interested in those topics know they can find like minds there. (One less benevolent example is that some law enforcement agencies claim that some people use IRC to exchange information about breaking into computers, or using stolen credit card numbers.)

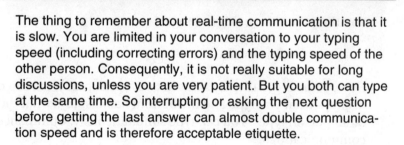

MAXIMIZING THE REAL-TIME SPEED LIMIT

The thing to remember about real-time communication is that it is slow. You are limited in your conversation to your typing speed (including correcting errors) and the typing speed of the other person. Consequently, it is not really suitable for long discussions, unless you are very patient. But you both can type at the same time. So interrupting or asking the next question before getting the last answer can almost double communication speed and is therefore acceptable etiquette.

talk, ntalk

Two main versions of the `talk` program are available on Internet systems: `talk` and `ntalk`. You use them the same way; however, `talk` might not successfully complete a link with `ntalk`, and vice versa.

Say you are working on your Internet system, the system beeps, and the following message appears:

```
Message from Talk_Daemon@well at 18:39 ...
```

```
talk: connection requested by drsmith@well.sf.ca.us.

talk: respond with:  talk drsmith@well.sf.ca.us
```

Note that the message tells you whether the sender is using talk or ntalk, and gives you the sender's user name and address.

First, write down the person's user name and address, because by the time you get out of what you are doing, that information may have scrolled off your screen.

Next, get out of what you are doing.

Then, type **talk *username@machinename.organization*** and press Enter. (If the other person is using ntalk, then type **ntalk** rather than talk.)

If the person is still logged in, you see the following message:

```
(Waiting for your party to respond)
```

You then should see this message:

```
(Connection established)
```

Here, your screen display splits in two, horizontally; the top half displays what you type and the bottom half displays what the other person types. You can type simultaneously. Commence communicating!

To exit talk or ntalk, type **^C**.

PUTTING THE BRAKES ON talk MESSAGES

You are under no obligation to respond to every talk message you receive, in the same way that you do not have to answer the telephone just because it rings. If you do not recognize the name, and you are busy right now or do not feel like entering into a real-time conversation, feel free to ignore the message.

If you want to disable incoming `talk` requests, type **mesg n** and press Enter. This shuts off incoming `talk` requests, unless they are in response to `talk` requests that you initiate. To reenable incoming `talk` requests, type **mesg y** and press Enter.

To initiate a `talk` request yourself, type the following:

talk *username@machinename.organization*

Then wait for the other person to respond. After a few moments with no response, `talk` replies with the following:

```
No answer. Ringing your party again.
```

It is considered bad manners to continue the attempt if the person does not respond. To stop the `talk` program from continuing to ring the other person, type **^c**.

Internet Relay Chat

Internet Relay Chat (IRC) is more of a way to communicate with more than one person on-line at a time, the equivalent of going to a party and finding separate rooms for discussions of politics, current events, and so on. Each "room" is called a *channel*. You might well find 500 or more people on IRC at a time. To run IRC, type **irc** and you are greeted by a screen like the one in figure 2.8.

```
*** ircII 2.1.5a - Welcome on the IRC!
***
*** Connecting to port 6667 of server rutishauser.stanford.edu
*** Welcome to the Internet Relay Network, slf
*** Your host is rutishauser.Stanford.EDU, running version 2.7.2h
*** If you have not already done so, please read the new user information with
+/HELP NEWUSER
*** This server was created Fri Apr 9 1993 at 08:56:23 PDT
-rutishauser.Stanford.EDU- There are 1292 users and 474 invisible on 163
+servers
-rutishauser.Stanford.EDU- 83 users have connection to the twilight zone
-rutishauser.Stanford.EDU- There are 466 channels.
-rutishauser.Stanford.EDU- I have 15 clients and 1 servers
-rutishauser.Stanford.EDU- MOTD - rutishauser.Stanford.EDU Message of the Day
+-
-rutishauser.Stanford.EDU- MOTD -
-rutishauser.Stanford.EDU- MOTD -                    Leland Stanford Junior
+University
-rutishauser.Stanford.EDU- MOTD -                              IRC Server
-rutishauser.Stanford.EDU- MOTD -
-rutishauser.Stanford.EDU- MOTD -              Rutishauser.Stanford.EDU
[ircII] slf --- more --- * type /help for help
>
ALT-F10   HELP   ANSI-BBS   FDX   2400 N81   LOG CLOSED   PRT OFF   CR     CR
```

Figure 2.8:

The IRC welcome screen.

IRC commands are all prefaced with /.

Type /**list** and press Enter to see what channels have been defined and the number of people using each one. In addition, some channels include descriptions of the topic under discussion (see fig. 2.9).

```
*** #ramone     1
*** #DDK        1
*** #u&me       2
*** #dpf        1      Let's get this baby off the ground...
*** #X11        3      Xlib, Xaw, Motif, XView, Tcl/Tk
*** #ne-raves   1
*** #Boston     1      The E. Massachusetts Metro Area + beyond!! :)
*** #Dominion   1
*** #latinos    3
*** #tlt        1
*** #forest     1
*** #MuscleBea  1
*** #p/g!       2
*** #tiger      1
*** #blf        1
*** #Serbia     1
*** #SkinnyPup  1
*** #Ministry   1
*** #bleagh     3      Narwhales?
*** #naroc      4
*** #2ez        2

[ircII] slf --- more --- * type /help for help
>
 ALT-F10  HELP | ANSI-BBS | FDX |  2400 N81 | LOG CLOSED | PRT OFF | CR  |  CR
```

Figure 2.9:

IRC channels in use.

To join a particular channel, type /**join** *channelname* (be sure to include the # in the channel name) and press Enter. You see what the other participants in that channel are typing, and you can participate in the discussion yourself by typing in your views.

To see what users are on your channel, type /**who** * and press Enter (see fig. 2.10).

To leave IRC, type /**exit**.

If you participate in a conversation, it is considered polite to tell the other participants you are leaving, in the same way that you say goodbye to people you talk with at a party, rather than abruptly leave.

To find out about other IRC commands, type /**help** and press Enter.

```
-rutishauser.Stanford.EDU- MOTD -        James Lambers (Augustus)
+lambers@sccn.Stanford.EDU
-rutishauser.Stanford.EDU- MOTD -        Bob Vaughan (techie)
+irc@w6yx.Stanford.EDU
-rutishauser.Stanford.EDU- MOTD -
-rutishauser.Stanford.EDU- * End of /MOTD command.
*** slf has joined channel #startrek
*** Topic: A dull night in startrek land....
*** InzadiBot has joined channel #startrek
Channel    Nickname  S  User@Host (Name)
#startrek   InzadiBot H  weathej@jacobs.CSOS.ORST.EDU (4 Where's Trake? :)
#startrek   slf       H  slf@netcom2.netcom.com (0 Sharon Fisher)
#startrek   MoMar     H@ gratien@lictor.acsu.buffalo.edu (4 Queen of Men)
#startrek   dougpaul  H@ dougpaul@140.174.87.1 (2 !id The Lionhearted)
#startrek   Admiral   H  tfarrell@lynx.dac.northeastern.edu (4 Thomas Farrell)
#startrek   Inzadi    H@ weathej@jacobs.CSOS.ORST.EDU (4 Where's Trake? :)
#startrek   Enterbot  H@ cs922044@iris.ariel.yorku.ca (8 !id Protector of the
+Star Trek Universe)
#startrek   slade     H@ nuttallp@helium.GAS.UUG.Arizona.EDU (3 slade)
#startrek   WorfBot   H@ nuttallp@helium.GAS.UUG.Arizona.EDU (2 !id WorfBot)
#startrek   Computer  H@ veikko@elaine44.Stanford.EDU (1 Nix)

[ircII] slf on #startrek (+tn) * type /help for help
#startrek>
ALT-F10  HELP   ANSI-BBS   FDX   2400 N81   LOG CLOSED   PRT OFF   CR    CR
```

Figure 2.10:

IRC users on a channel.

MUDs, MUSEs, and Other Strange Things

MUDs (Multiuser Dungeons), MUSEs (Multiuser Simulation Environments), and so on, are a strange category. Technically, they are games—role-playing games. If you have ever played a game such as Dungeons and Dragons, you know what a role-playing game is. However, if you have played such games to any extent, you know that the game often becomes more than "just a game" to the participants.

This is especially true in the case of MUDs (or MUSEs—the terms are essentially interchangeable). Although they indeed enable you to wander around a defined space and gather materials and so on, the "gather treasure and kill monsters" aspect of traditional role-playing games can be greatly downplayed in favor of communication, working together, and setting up societies. People often use MUDs to see what it would be like to act as a different character—a man rather than a woman, a warrior rather than a computer programmer, and so on. MUDs are often based on works of science fiction or fantasy.

Some MUDs enable you to sign up for a character on the fly and register that character yourself; others require that you send e-mail to a *wizard*, a person in charge of running the game, and the wizard defines a character and e-mails it back to you.

CAUTION

DON'T PLAY ALL DAY

Some Internet providers do not permit you to run MUDs, or allow them only during certain hours of the day. Similarly, some MUDs have restricted hours. In any case, it is not a good idea to tie up a machine for many hours during busy parts of the day playing MUDs.

Learning More about MUDs

You can learn more about MUDs from a number of Netnews groups that cover them, such as `rec.games.mud`. For example, a FAQ gets posted to `rec.games.mud` periodically, explaining the concepts behind them and some basic guidelines for behavior.

To get guidelines and help for a specific MUD, you need to join that MUD and type **help**.

People already on the MUD can be helpful. When you log on to a MUD, it often tells you who you can ask for help. Keep in mind that the more popular the game, the less willing players might be to help a new person along, because they don't want to end up spending all their time helping new players while getting little time to play themselves. At the same time, without a critical mass of players on-line at a time, the game can never really take off. Even the popular games can be slow-moving, especially if you are new and don't know the people.

Finding MUDs

A list of MUDs is posted periodically to the Netnews group `rec.games.mud.announce`. Note that each one has a port number. The *port number* is the specific "entrance" designated for MUDs on that machine. The list also notes restrictions for each MUD, plus ways to obtain more information or register for a character.

Joining and Leaving MUDs

You can log in to a MUD using the `telnet` command, described in more detail in Chapter 3. Generally, though, it works as follows:

```
telnet machinename.organization portnumber
```

You then press Enter, and are automatically logged in to the MUD.

In addition, MUD players have written other programs specifically designed for running MUDs. An example of such a program is tf, or tinyfugue, described in more detail in the MUD FAQ. If such programs are available on your system, they offer an easier-to-use interface to the world of MUDs.

The standard command for exiting a MUD is quit or logout.

Summary

Now you should know the basics of communicating with other individuals on the computer, such as e-mail, including ways to send e-mail to other systems, ways to deal with problems, basic real-time conversational programs, and some familiarity with MUDs. The next chapter discusses ways to log on to other Internet machines and retrieve data from them.

CHAPTER 3

Connecting with Other Computers

If you are the type of person who especially likes bulletin boards and other on-line services because of the neat software you find there, this chapter is for you. In that sense, the Internet is the biggest bulletin board in the world. Hundreds of sites exist on the Internet, each with at least as much software as any BBS you have ever seen.

You also can log in to other computers to get other kinds of information stored there, not just software. Increasingly, national, state, and local governments are storing data on systems on the Internet, for use by their constituents. Companies and organizations do so as well. And, of course, the Internet is one of the largest repositories of information on the Internet itself.

In addition, you may want to log in to other computers to make use of resources found there, such as special printers or games.

This chapter discusses the following:

→ Logging in to another computer

→ Logging out from a system

→ Using systems responsibly

→ Finding other computers to log in to

→ Using the file transfer protocol (ftp)

→ Downloading files from the Internet to your PC

Logging In to Another Computer

The Internet gives you the capability of logging in to any other computer on the Internet that permits it. (For example, you can send electronic mail to the president at a site called whitehouse.gov, but you cannot log in to that system.)

Later in this chapter you will learn about two commands that enable you to log in to a remote computer. These commands are rlogin and telnet.

The rlogin command is most often used by a user who has an account on two different machines to move back and forth between them. Also, some commands and services are available only to users who are either logged in correctly or using rlogin. If you have an account on the system you are connecting to, you probably will want to use rlogin to make the connection. It is possible to use rlogin to make connections to guest accounts on other machines, although telnet generally is the more useful command in this situation.

By convention, the command telnet usually is used to enable you to connect to the computer systems for which you do not have an account of your own. It is possible, however, to use telnet in making a connection into another registered account on a remote machine. When you use the telnet command to make the connection, you actually are running a program called telnet and running under the telnet protocol. This just means that things are getting done a little differently than with the rlogin command. These differences will be invisible to you, so rlogin and telnet will seem very similar. Either command probably will make the connection you want.

If you are getting e-mail and Netnews on one system, what would be the point of logging in to another system? The reason is for the services offered by that system. Systems such as the Byte Information Exchange (BIX) and the WELL, for example, offer conferencing over and above their Internet connections. By logging in to an Internet system near you, you can take advantage of the services on these other systems without having to dial them directly (although you do need accounts on those machines before taking advantage of most of their features).

In addition, if you travel, the ability to log in to other computers over the Internet means that you can log in to a system while away, and keep up with your e-mail and Netnews at the same time. Many computer shows, for example, are now featuring clusters of terminals specifically for this purpose.

Other services that you can use by logging in to a remote computer include data repositories at universities and educational institutions around the world. Remember that the Internet originally was set up for research; many such institutions are connected! You can get information such as access to library card catalogs, bibliographic databases, and government publications for foreign countries as well as the United States.

TIP

Remember that only sites with full Internet connections will let you log in remotely.

How To Use rlogin

The rlogin command assumes you are logging in to the other system with the same user name under which you are currently logged in to your system. Consequently, the remote system automatically logs you in under that user name, and then prompts you for a password, as shown in figure 3.1.

The {Netcom:9} in the first line of figure 3.1 is the prompt on the machine you originally logged in to. This section is about the rlogin well.sf.ca.us command. The next line is the remote machine requesting a password. As you probably can guess, the rlogin was successful in this example, and the rest of the figure shows what the remote machine sent back after the connection was made. The important thing to note about this example is that the user did not specify which account on the remote machine to log in to. Because no account was specified, the remote machine assumed the account name would be the same as the one in which the connection was made from.

```
{Netcom:9} rlogin well.sf.ca.us
Password:
Last login: Mon Jun 21 19:19:57 from netcom2.netcom.c

          DYNIX(R) V3.1.4 NFS  #2 (): Tue Mar 31 12:38:27 PST 1992
          =========================================================

     You own your own words. This means that you are responsible for the
     words that you post on the WELL and that reproduction of those words
     without your permission in any medium outside of the WELL's conferencing
     system may be challenged by you, the author.

     The WELL is unavailable during backups each Sunday from 2am until 5:30am.

     Thanks for dropping into the WELL.


You have mail.




ALT-F10  HELP  | ANSI-BBS | FDX |  4800 N81 | LOG CLOSED | PRT OFF | CR   |   CR
```

Figure 3.1:

Connecting to another machine by rlogin.

You also can use rlogin with another user name by specifying it with the -1 flag, as follows, then pressing Enter:

        rlogin *machinename.organization* -1 *username*

An example is shown in figure 3.2:

```
{Netcom:11} rlogin netcom.netcom.com -1 sharon
Password:
Last login: Mon Jun 21 18:54:52 from netcom2

SunOS Release 4.1.3 (NETCOM) #1: Wed Sep 23 05:06:55 PDT 1992

NETCOM On-line Communication Services, Inc.

   >>>>
   >>>>    PORTLAND POP Now on-line (503) 626-6833
   >>>>
   >>>>    IRVINE POP Now On-line (714) 708-3800
   >>>>
   >>>>    SJ PEP was (408) 241-9902, is  now (408) 241-9903
   >>>>
You have new mail.
We have not received your Internet agreement forms within the grace period.
Please call the office (408) 554-8649.




ALT-F10  HELP  | ANSI-BBS | FDX |  4800 N81 | LOG CLOSED | PRT OFF | CR   |   CR
```

Figure 3.2:

Connecting to another machine with another user name by using rlogin.

The important difference between figures 3.2 and 3.1 is on the first line. In figure 3.2, the -1 flag is used to tell the remote machine what account you want to log in to. As in figure 3.1, the rest of the figure shows what appears on the screen after the connection is made.

One of the differences between telnet and rlogin is that with the `rlogin` command information about the type of terminal you are emulating automatically is transferred to the remote system. Unless you are emulating a particularly unusual type of terminal, this usually is not important.

To get more information about the `rlogin` command, type the following, and press Enter:

```
man rlogin
```

GETTING LOST CAN COST MONEY

CAUTION

If you are moving between multiple sites using telnet or rlogin, remember where you are. If sometimes you start from one system, and then remotely log in to the other, and sometimes you start from the other system, you could forget where you are and set up multiple, overlapping telnet or rlogin sessions. This slows down your performance and, if you are paying for your login time, costs you money.

How To Use telnet

The `telnet` command is the original, classic command for logging in to another computer. This is the way the command is typed:

```
telnet machinename.organization
```

It is followed by pressing Enter, where `machinename.organization` is the name of the machine and its domain address.

With some systems, you will need to use the numerical Internet address, as shown in some of the entries in table 3.1 later in this chapter. In that case, the command is in this form:

`telnet` *`numericInternetaddress`*

You then press Enter. Note that the *numericInternetaddress*, also known as the *IP Number*, has four individual numbers separated by periods and no spaces.

TRICKS FOR MAKING A CONNECTION

Sometimes not all machines know how to reach all other machines. Although Netcom knows how to reach BIX, some Internet systems do not and will respond to your `telnet` request with *`machinename.organization`*: `unknown host`. If this happens, try using the four-number Internet address, if you have it. Or, if you have accounts on multiple systems, try your request from one of those other systems.

After the `telnet` command links to the other system, you can log in to that system. You may already know how to log in, perhaps by using a guest account—or the remote system may give you instructions, as shown in figure 3.3.

```
{Netcom:3} telnet well.sf.ca.us
Trying...
Connected to well.sf.ca.us.
Escape character is '^]'.


This is The WELL

DYNIX(R) V3.1.0  (well)

Type     newuser     to sign up.
Type     trouble     if you are having trouble logging in.
Type     guest       to learn about The WELL.

If you already have a WELL account, type your username.

login: slf
Password:




ALT-F10   HELP  | ANSI-BBS | FDX  |  4800 N81 | LOG CLOSED | PRT OFF | CR  |  CR
```

Figure 3.3:

Using `telnet` to connect to another system.

After you are logged in to the other system, you use it just as though you were logged in directly.

In addition, you can enter the `telnet` command, which activates the telnet program, and issue commands from within it by typing the following and pressing Enter:

> `telnet`

To initiate a link with another system from within the telnet program, type **open**, along with the machine name or address, as in the following, then press Enter:

> **open** `machinename.organization`

Or you can type the following:

> **open** `numericInternetaddress`

An example is shown in figure 3.4.

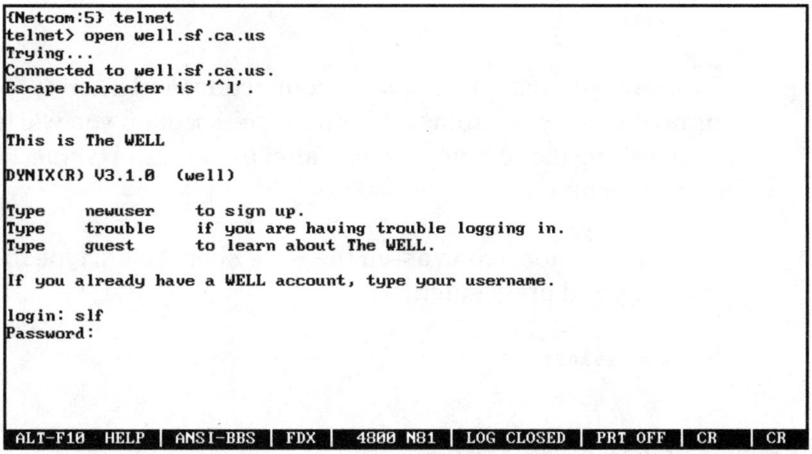

```
{Netcom:5} telnet
telnet> open well.sf.ca.us
Trying...
Connected to well.sf.ca.us.
Escape character is '^]'.


This is The WELL

DYNIX(R) V3.1.0  (well)

Type     newuser      to sign up.
Type     trouble      if you are having trouble logging in.
Type     guest        to learn about The WELL.

If you already have a WELL account, type your username.

login: slf
Password:




ALT-F10  HELP  |  ANSI-BBS  |  FDX  |  4800 N81  |  LOG CLOSED  |  PRT OFF  |  CR  |  CR
```

Figure 3.4:

Using another system with the `telnet` command.

A telnet TRICK

Even if the remote machine is down or you cannot make the connection for some reason, the telnet program remains active until you exit it. Whether you use the "telnet machine" form of the command or the `telnet` command alone, followed by an open command, if a connection fails, you still will be running the telnet program. You know this for sure because your prompt has changed to:

```
telnet>
```

You might want to close a connection and remain in telnet so that you can open another. To close a telnet connection without exiting from telnet, type the following at the `telnet>` prompt, and press Enter:

close *machinename@organization*

To exit the `telnet` command, type the following and press Enter:

exit

The `close` command just closes a connection, and the `exit` command just exits from telnet. In the next section you will learn about exiting the remote machine after a successful connection has been made.

To get more information about the `telnet` command, type the following, and press Enter:

man telnet

Logging Out from the System

Depending on whether you logged in to the system from within the `telnet` command, or made a direct connection, you may need to log out from the remote system before you exit from telnet.

The correct command for logging out of the other system varies. Examples include:

```
exit
quit
bye
logout
```
holding down the Ctrl key and pressing c

Note that the remote system to which you are connected may not be a Unix system, and may not respond the way you expect it to. It could be an IBM mainframe, for example, and expect your PC to emulate an IBM 3270 terminal. In this case, your PC may not be capable of sending the sort of signals that the remote computer expects. Or, if you are remotely logging in to something such as a card catalog, the system may be designed for use from public terminals, from which users do not log out.

If your computer locks up, the ^] character (which you send by holding down the Ctrl key and pressing the] key) will generally return you to the telnet prompt, at which point you can close the connection, or exit from telnet.

At worst, you can exit your communications program or hang up your modem connection.

When you log in to a remote machine using telnet, it often will tell you how to log out. Read those directions and avoid guessing the command at the end of your session.

Using Systems Responsibly

It is important to remember that the institutions and organizations providing these services are doing you a favor. They go to considerable expense to make these facilities available to the Internet population, and the needs of their constituents must always come first.

Consequently, you need to use these facilities with courtesy and consideration, as suggested in the following:

➡ Avoid using them during local business hours or during busy periods, such as during university final exams.

→ Do not tie up connections for long periods of time. These organizations and institutions often limit the number of guest users, and your using the line means that others cannot.

→ Do not copy large amounts of data simply because it's available; make sure that you really need the data you transfer. Some graphic files, for example, can be hundreds of thousands of bytes long.

→ Try to find another site if a particular site is frequently busy, or if its network connection is not high-speed. Information is often available at more than one site.

→ Try to break large amounts of information into several groups of information so that you can obtain what you need through several sessions.

→ If a site refuses connections to guest users, find another site or try to connect at a another time, rather than complain. Remember that you are a guest.

Finding Other Computers To Log In To

Like special little restaurants, the locations of many computers that allow guest logins are passed around by word of mouth. If you are looking for some particular service, the place to start is in Netnews groups and mailing lists that discuss that type of service. The FAQ (Frequently Asked Questions) list for those Netnews groups and mailing lists may give you some information. In addition, references to and lists of such sites may be posted to the Netnews groups and mailing lists periodically. Also, sites may have information on other sites.

A rather extensive list of services is published periodically to Netnews, in the `alt.bbs.internet` newsgroup, as the `Services` list. It's worth getting a copy of, even if only to browse through and familiarize yourself with the rich variety of information resources.

Other interesting systems include those shown in table 3.1.

Organization	Address
Library of Congress	192.65.218.43 or dra.com
Dartmouth on-line catalogs and databases	129.170.16.11
CARL database of Internet resources	192.54.81.128
Rutgers University	info.rutgers.edu
University of California, Berkeley	infocal.berkeley.edu
The WELL conferencing system	well.sf.ca.us
The BIX conferencing system	x25.bix.com

Table 3.1

A Sampling of Internet Services

For more information on finding other computers to log in to, see Chapter 5.

Using the File Transfer Protocol (ftp)

If you have uploaded programs to or downloaded programs from an on-line service before, you know that you use a special feature of your communications software to do so. This software communicates with software on the on-line service, which breaks up the program into manageable pieces, then sends the pieces one at a time, checking to make sure that the software on the receiving end of the connection has received each piece before sending another one.

The same is true between two computers on the Internet, except that the software is called *File Transfer Protocol*, or ftp. Ftp is a much faster way of exchanging data than any other method, such as e-mail. This section explains how to use ftp between your Internet account and other systems, both with individual accounts and guest accounts.

ADVICE FOR DOWNLOADING

Remember, if you are downloading files to your account on an Internet system, you still need to use the communications software file transfer or logging feature on your PC to upload or download data or software between your account on the Internet system and your PC. See "Downloading Files from the Internet to Your PC," later in this chapter.

Connecting to Another System with ftp

As with telnet and rlogin, ftp gives you two different ways to connect to a remote system—either as part of issuing the `ftp` command or from within ftp.

To connect to a remote system while issuing the `ftp` command, type the following, and press Enter:

> ftp *machinename@organization*

If the connection is made, the remote system responds with its welcome message, as shown in figure 3.5.

```
{Netcom:5} ftp well.sf.ca.us
Connected to well.sf.ca.us.
220 well FTP server (BU 5.84 (from UUNET 5.51) Wed Nov 25 17:10:31 PST 1992) rea
dy.
Name (well.sf.ca.us:slf):
331 Password required for slf.
Password:
230 User slf logged in.
ftp>
```

```
ALT-F10  HELP  |  ANSI-BBS  |  FDX  |  4800 N81  |  LOG CLOSED  |  PRT OFF  |  CR  |    CR
```

Figure 3.5:

Setting up an ftp connection (netcom to netcom, or well to netcom).

To connect to a remote system from within the `ftp` command, type the following, and press Enter:

    ftp

Then type the following, and press Enter:

    open *machinename@organization*

If the connection is made, the remote system responds with its welcome message, as shown in figure 3.6.

```
{Netcom:7} ftp
ftp> open well.sf.ca.us
Connected to well.sf.ca.us.
220 well FTP server (BU 5.84 (from UUNET 5.51) Wed Nov 25 17:10:31 PST 1992) rea
dy.
Name (well.sf.ca.us:slf):
331 Password required for slf.
Password:
230 User slf logged in.
ftp>




ALT-F10   HELP  │ ANSI-BBS │ FDX │  4800 N81 │ LOG CLOSED │ PRT OFF │ CR │   CR
```

Figure 3.6:

Setting up a connection from within ftp (netcom to netcom, or well to netcom).

ERROR MESSAGE INFO

As with telnet and rlogin, the system on which you have your Internet account may not be capable of setting up the connection if it does not know about the other system. If so, ftp responds with the following error message:

    machinename.organization: unknown host

If you receive this message, try using the four-number Internet address, if you have it. Or, if you have accounts on multiple systems, try your request from one of those other systems.

After the `telnet` command links to the other system, you can log in to it and begin transferring files.

TIP

ftp TRICKS

If you use ftp to connect directly to another machine, rather than run the `ftp` command and then open your connection, you may be sent to within the `ftp` command if your request fails. You will know that you are within the `ftp` command if your command prompt changes to:

```
ftp>
```

To close an ftp connection without exiting from ftp, type the following at the `ftp` prompt and press Enter:

close *machinename@organization*

To exit from ftp, type the following at the `ftp` prompt, and press Enter:

quit

To find out what you can do in ftp, see "Finding ftp Sites and Services" and the sections following it in this chapter.

Using anonymous ftp

The main reason people use ftp is not to log in to individual accounts on other Internet systems, but to use guest accounts with free software and data that have been set up all over the world. Because these accounts usually are set up for logging in under the name *anonymous*, the process is referred to as anonymous ftp, although the ftp is the same.

anonymous ADVICE

Not all Internet systems that support ftp connections also support anonymous ftp. Do not attempt to log in anonymously to a random Internet system in hopes of striking pay dirt; the system administrator at the remote site may not take kindly to your attempts. In addition, some Internet systems have separate Internet addresses set up specifically for anonymous ftp. If you are using anonymous ftp, be sure that you are using the correct address.

To log in to a remote system's anonymous ftp repository or archive, first determine what the guest account login is. Usually, it is **anonymous**. The login process looks as shown in figure 3.7.

```
{Netcom:3} ftp ftp.nisc.sri.com
Connected to phoebus.NISC.SRI.COM.
220-*** This is the SRI NISC FTP host.  Login with username "anonymous" ***
220-*** and your e-mail address as the password.  The following         ***
220-*** directories are available:                                      ***
220-
220-     rfc and fyi -      All the online RFCs and FYIs
220-     ien -              Internet Engineering Notes
220-     iesg -             Minutes from the IETF Steering Group
220-     ietf -             Minutes from IETF working groups
220-     netinfo -          General informational files on the Internet
220-     internet-drafts -  Drafts on standards from the IETF working groups.
220-     pub -              General information
220-     bboard-archives -  Archives for tcp-ip, namedroppers and cisco
220-
220 phoebus FTP server (Version 2.0WU(10) Mon Apr 19 11:29:24 PDT 1993) ready.
Name (ftp.nisc.sri.com:slf): anonymous
331 Guest login ok, send your complete e-mail address as password.
Password:
230 Guest login ok, access restrictions apply.
ftp>

ALT-F10  HELP | ANSI-BBS | FDX | 4800 N81 | LOG CLOSED | PRT OFF | CR | CR
```

Figure 3.7:

Anonymously logging in to an ftp repository.

Notice that the remote system prompts you to enter your own Internet address as the password. This is so that the network administrator of the remote system can keep a record of who is using the repository. The remote system does not check to see whether the information you enter is correct, but it is courteous of you to enter the correct information. Network administrators faced with a large number of untraceable users may decide not to continue to offer this privilege.

Finding anonymous ftp Sites

As with Internet systems that permit guest logins, the locations of computers that permit anonymous ftp locations are passed by word-of-mouth. If you are looking for some particular data or program, the place to start is in Netnews groups and mailing lists that discuss that type of data or program. The FAQ (Frequently Asked Questions) list for those Netnews groups and mailing lists may give you some information. In addition, references to and lists of such sites may be posted to the Netnews groups and mailing lists periodically, and sites themselves may have information on other sites.

Other interesting systems include the ones shown in table 3.2.

Table 3.2

Available Services
and Systems

Information Available	Address
Macintosh software	`sumex-aim.stanford.edu` `mac.archive.umich.edu`
Weather maps	`unidata.ucar.edu` in images `aurelie.soest.hawaii.edu1` in images
European weather maps	`cumulus.met.ed.ac.uk` in images/gifs
Political data	`ftp.css.itd.umich.edu` `redspread.css.itd.umich.edu`
The Electronic Library	`ftp.law.columbia.edu`

IBM PC Software	`wsmr-simtel20.army.mil`
	`oak.oakland.edu`
	`plains.nodak.edu`

PC software	`wuarchive.wustl.edu`

Information about the Internet	`ftp.nisc.sri.com`
	`cnri.reston.va.us`
	`nis.merit.edu`

For more information on finding other computers to log in to, see Chapter 5.

LOOK BEFORE YOU DOWNLOAD

CAUTION

Before you start downloading files from other systems, keep in mind that some of these files, such as graphic gif files, can be large and can take a long time to download to your PC. If you are charged for disk space (or even if you aren't charged), check the size of a file before you download it, and be sure to delete files promptly from your Internet account when you are finished with them.

Finding ftp Sites and Services

Moving around within an Internet system's ftp area is actually not very different from using DOS, if that is any consolation. As with DOS, files are organized into directories. To move to another directory, use the **cd** command, as shown in figure 3.8.

```
-rw-r--r--   1 root     daemon     226319 Apr 27 22:42 INDEX
drwxrwsr-x   5 root     staff         512 Jul 30  1992 bboard-archives
drwxr-sr-x   2 root     staff         512 Apr 20 06:23 bin
drwxr-sr-x   2 root     staff         512 Mar  1 06:56 dev
drwxr-sr-x   2 root     staff        2048 Apr 21 20:17 etc
lrwxrwxrwx   1 root     daemon          3 Mar  1 04:08 fyi -> rfc
drwxr-xr-x   2 root     daemon       3072 Nov 13  1991 ien
drwxrwsr-x   2 root     ftp-writ     2048 Jun 20 03:11 iesg
drwxrwsr-x128 gvaudre   ftp-writ     3072 Jun 20 03:11 ietf
drwxr-xr-x   2 root     staff         512 Jun  7 17:10 incoming
lrwxrwxrwx   1 root     daemon          5 Mar  1 04:02 index -> INDEX
drwsrwsr-x   2 gvaudre  ftp-writ    32256 Jun 20 03:12 internet-drafts
drwxrwxr-x   2 root     staff         512 Nov  3  1992 introducing.the.internet
drwxr-xr-x   2 root     wheel        8192 Feb 28 21:16 lost+found
drwxrwsr-x   3 root     staff        1536 May 14 22:34 netinfo
drwxr-xr-x   4 root     daemon        512 Jun  4 20:09 outgoing
drwsrwxr-x   6 root     staff         512 Feb  7 03:41 pub
drwxrwsr-x   2 rfc      ftp-writ    18944 Jun 16 05:46 rfc
drwxr-xr-x   3 root     staff         512 Apr 18  1991 usr
226 Transfer complete.
1220 bytes received in 0.61 seconds (2 Kbytes/s)
ftp> cd pub
250 CWD command successful.
ftp>
ALT-F10  HELP  | ANSI-BBS | FDX |  4800 N81 | LOG CLOSED | PRT OFF | CR  |  CR
```

Figure 3.8:

Using the **cd** command to change a directory (see lower left corner).

To move back up to the previous directory, type the following and press Enter:

    cd ..

To find out what files are located in the current directory, type the following and press Enter:

    dir

You will see something similar to what is shown in figure 3.9.

```
Password:
230 Guest login ok, access restrictions apply.
ftp> dir
200 PORT command successful.
150 ASCII data connection for /bin/ls (192.100.81.108,3401) (0 bytes).
total 61
-rw-rw-rw-  1 0        0                84 Jun 19 06:20 NULL
dr-xr-sr-x  2 0        5000            512 Aug  8  1989 bin
dr-xr-sr-x  2 0        5000            512 Apr 23  1991 dev
drwxrwxr-x  2 1100     1001           1536 Jun 18 15:24 iesg
drwxrwxr-x135 1100     1001          20480 Jun 21 15:34 ietf
drwxr-xr-x102 1100     1001           3584 Jun 21 17:28 ietf-mail-archive
drwxrwsr-x  2 1100     1001          16896 Jun 21 17:55 internet-drafts
drwxrwxr-x  8 1030     1003           1024 May 19 23:16 isoc
drwxr-xr-x  2 1057     1000            512 Jun 16 14:46 jgrass
drwxr-xr-x  2 0        0              8192 Apr 19  1991 lost+found
drwxrwxr-x  2 1013     1               512 Sep 27  1991 rdroms
drwxrwxr-x  2 1017     1000            512 Nov 18  1991 temp
drwxrwxr-x  2 1038     1               512 Feb 24 13:44 titd
drwxr-xr-x  2 0        1               512 Mar 26 22:04 us_users
dr-xr-sr-x  4 0        5000            512 Aug 17  1992 usr
226 ASCII Transfer complete.
945 bytes received in 0.56 seconds (1.6 Kbytes/s)
ftp>
ALT-F10  HELP │ ANSI-BBS │ FDX │ 4800 N81 │ LOG CLOSED │ PRT OFF │  CR  │  CR
```

Figure 3.9:

Files found in an
ftp directory.

To get more information about the particular ftp archive you are using, look for files with names such as index or read.me and download them first (see next section).

Downloading Text Files with ftp

To download a particular file, type the following and press Enter:

    get *filename*

The system will respond with something similar to what is shown in figure 3.10.

If you want to name the file something else on your PC, type:

    get *filename PCfilename*

If the file is a directory, you cannot download it. Directories have a d as the first character in their list of attributes, such as this:

    drwxr-sr-x 2 root   staff   512 Apr 20 06:23 bin

If you try to download a directory, ftp responds with:

```
550 filename: not a plain file
```

Note that the get command does not show you the information in
the file as it is downloaded. You need to go back to your local
Internet system and read the files there. Sometimes, for such files
as indices and read.me, you may want to read them while in your ftp
session. In that case, download the files with the - option, as follows:

```
get filename -
```

Then press Enter. The - sends the information to the screen
rather than downloading it to your local Internet system.

```
-rw-rw-r--   1 vivian    ftp-writ    23566 Jul  7  1992 mail_methods
-rw-r--r--   1 vivian    staff        1839 Aug  3  1992 may-92-update-contents
-rw-r--r--   1 vivian    staff        5275 Dec  1  1992 memberlist
-rw-rw-r--   1 vivian    ftp-writ    12141 Jan 22  1992 network-map-locations
-rw-rw-r--   1 vivian    staff        9492 Apr  2 21:58 nic-pubs.txt
-rw-rw-r--   1 vivian    staff        5687 May 14 22:13 nisc-pubs.txt
-rw-r--r--   1 vivian    staff        3214 Jun  2  1992 nsfnet-stats.info
lrwxrwxrwx   1 vivian    staff          20 Mar  1 04:02 nsfnet.policy -> POLICY/ns
fnet.policy
-rw-rw-r--   1 vivian    ftp-writ   513329 Sep  4  1992 old-interest-groups
-rw-rw-r--   1 vivian    ftp-writ    90112 Apr  5  1991 policies.tar
-rw-rw-r--   1 vivian    staff          59 Aug 18  1992 rfc-sets.txt
-rw-rw-r--   1 vivian    ftp-writ   160269 Mar  8  1991 security-doc.txt
-rw-rw-r--   1 vivian    ftp-writ   369605 Feb 11  1992 vendors-guide.doc
-rw-rw-r--   1 vivian    ftp-writ     3248 May 11  1992 vendors-template.doc
226 Transfer complete.
2769 bytes received in 0.42 seconds (6.4 Kbytes/s)
ftp> get nisc-pubs.txt
200 PORT command successful.
150 Opening ASCII mode data connection for nisc-pubs.txt (5687 bytes).
226 Transfer complete.
local: nisc-pubs.txt remote: nisc-pubs.txt
5800 bytes received in 0.17 seconds (33 Kbytes/s)
ftp>
ALT-F10  HELP | ANSI-BBS | FDX | 4800 N81 | LOG CLOSED | PRT OFF | CR | CR
```

Figure 3.10:
Downloading a file
with ftp (see lower
left corner for
ftp>get misc-
pubs.txt).

Downloading Multiple Files

If you want to download more than one file at a time, you could
simply use the get command for each file individually, or use the
mget command. This stands for "multiple get" and you can use it
with wild cards the same way that you can with a PC system. If,
for example, you want all the files with the extension .txt from a
particular directory, make your connection to the remote ftp
system, type the following, and press Enter:

```
mget *.txt
```

The system responds as shown in figure 3.11.

```
-rw-rw-r--   1 vivian    ftp-writ    513329 Sep  4  1992 old-interest-groups
-rw-rw-r--   1 vivian    ftp-writ     90112 Apr  5  1991 policies.tar
-rw-rw-r--   1 vivian    staff           59 Aug 18  1992 rfc-sets.txt
-rw-rw-r--   1 vivian    ftp-writ    160269 Mar  8  1991 security-doc.txt
-rw-rw-r--   1 vivian    ftp-writ    369605 Feb 11  1992 vendors-guide.doc
-rw-rw-r--   1 vivian    ftp-writ      3248 May 11  1992 vendors-template.doc
226 Transfer complete.
2769 bytes received in 0.29 seconds (9.3 Kbytes/s)
ftp> mget *.txt
mget country_codes.txt? n
mget ddn-mgt-bulletin-92.txt? y
200 PORT command successful.
150 Opening ASCII mode data connection for ddn-mgt-bulletin-92.txt (2792 bytes).
226 Transfer complete.
local: ddn-mgt-bulletin-92.txt remote: ddn-mgt-bulletin-92.txt
2850 bytes received in 0.086 seconds (32 Kbytes/s)
mget ddn-mgt-bulletin-99.txt? n
mget ddn-news-index.txt? y
200 PORT command successful.
150 Opening ASCII mode data connection for ddn-news-index.txt (6231 bytes).
226 Transfer complete.
local: ddn-news-index.txt remote: ddn-news-index.txt
6334 bytes received in 0.3 seconds (21 Kbytes/s)
mget gosip-order-info.txt?
ALT-F10  HELP | ANSI-BBS | FDX |  4800 N81 | LOG CLOSED | PRT OFF | CR | CR
```

Figure 3.11:

Downloading multiple files with mget (see the ninth line down, for starters).

The system asks you if you want each file. To tell ftp that you want the file, type **y**, and press Enter. If you do not want the file, type **n** and press Enter.

If you want all the files that your wild card indicates, you can turn this prompt off by typing **prompt** at the ftp> prompt before typing the mget command. To turn the prompt back on, type **prompt** again.

Downloading Programs with ftp

If you are downloading software, graphics, or some other data that is stored in binary rather than ASCII form, you need to tell ftp that you are downloading the file in binary form. To do this, use the binary command:

binary get *filename*

Then press Enter after each command.

ASCII VS. BINARY FILES

Unless you use the binary command, ftp will assume that you are working with ASCII or text files consisting of letters, numbers, and other ASCII characters. Other files, like executable programs, would look like garbage if you printed them. These files are called binary files and are handled by the system in a different way.

Before downloading text files or ASCII data again, use the `ascii` command to turn off the binary method of handling files:

```
ascii get filename
```

Then press Enter after each command.

HOW TO PROTECT AGAINST VIRUSES

If you are downloading programs from systems on the Internet, it is important that you obtain virus protection software and run it regularly—ideally, each time you log in, but at least every time you download a new program. Otherwise, you could download a program that could destroy all the data on your computer. The Internet is not any worse in this respect than any bulletin board—in fact, because some repositories insist on source code contributions, it may be safer than a local bulletin board—but you should not take any chances.

Compressing and Decompressing Files

Large files, such as programs, are often *compressed*, or stored in a way so that they take up less space and transmit more quickly. This means, however, that you will need to decompress them to use them. Compressed Unix files, for example, often have `.z` at the end of their names. (Compressed files also are stored in binary format; see the preceding `binary` command.)

In most cases, if the Internet system you are using has the decompress utility available, all you have to do to decompress the software for Unix is type the following and press Enter at the Internet system prompt (not the ftp prompt):

```
decompress filename
```

If this utility is not available, you need to ask the system administrator of your Internet site what command you should use.

On the other hand, software for the PC may be compressed with a utility called PKZIP, while software for the Macintosh may be converted into an ASCII format for transmission with a utility called BINHEX.

The compression document, which is available in the pcnet directory at the ftp site ftp.cso.uiuc.edu, gives a list of different ways that files can be compressed, how to compress and decompress them, and where to find the various kinds of compression software on the Internet.

Downloading Files from the Internet to Your PC

To run the downloaded software on your PC, you need to move the software a second time, from your Internet system account to your PC. The instructions for this vary depending on your PC's communications software (check your manuals) and on the types of downloading software offered by your Internet system.

You must have a communications package, running on your PC, to move the file from your Internet account to the PC. This might be Procomm, Crosstalk, or any other communication program. All of these programs support many different methods of moving the files. You will need to choose one of these methods that also is supported by the system in which you have your Internet account.

Kermit and XMODEM are very common and are supported almost anywhere. If you are not sure about which protocol to use in your communications package, choose one of these and it probably will work fine.

For example, this is what you would type to move a file from an Internet account on netcom to a PC, using XMODEM: (st stands for send text.)

```
xmodem st filename
```

XMODEM then responds by telling you to initiate the communications software on your PC, as shown in figure 3.12.

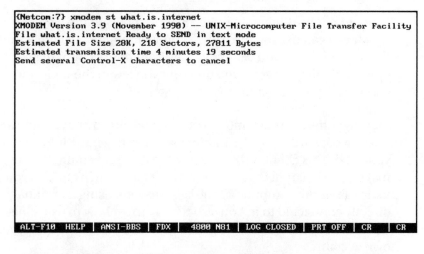

```
{Netcom:7} xmodem st what.is.internet
XMODEM Version 3.9 (November 1990) -- UNIX-Microcomputer File Transfer Facility
File what.is.internet Ready to SEND in text mode
Estimated File Size 28K, 218 Sectors, 27811 Bytes
Estimated transmission time 4 minutes 19 seconds
Send several Control-X characters to cancel
```

```
ALT-F10  HELP  | ANSI-BBS | FDX  |  4800 N81 | LOG CLOSED | PRT OFF | CR  |   CR
```

Figure 3.12:

Starting to download a file from an Internet system to your PC.

After you have started the software on your PC, XMODEM calculates how long it will take to download the software, and begins the process. (The calculation is only a rough one; do not take it as gospel.) This is shown in a box that will appear on your screen before the file is downloaded (see fig. 3.13).

Summary

At this point, you should have the basics of remotely logging in to another system on the Internet and of downloading data and programs from other Internet systems using ftp.

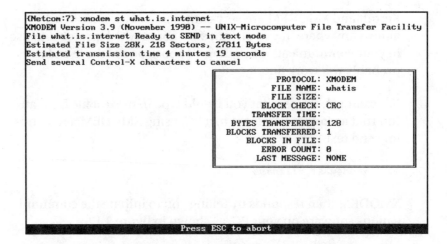

```
{Netcom:7} xmodem st what.is.internet
XMODEM Version 3.9 (November 1990) -- UNIX-Microcomputer File Transfer Facility
File what.is.internet Ready to SEND in text mode
Estimated File Size 28K, 218 Sectors, 27811 Bytes
Estimated transmission time 4 minutes 19 seconds
Send several Control-X characters to cancel
                                    PROTOCOL: XMODEM
                                   FILE NAME: whatis
                                   FILE SIZE:
                                 BLOCK CHECK: CRC
                               TRANSFER TIME:
                           BYTES TRANSFERRED: 128
                          BLOCKS TRANSFERRED: 1
                             BLOCKS IN FILE:
                                 ERROR COUNT: 0
                                LAST MESSAGE: NONE

                         Press ESC to abort
```

Figure 3.13:

Downloading a file from an Internet system to your PC.

It would not be difficult to write an entire book on the ways in which you can use the Internet to connect remote machines, and the ways in which you can move files from one account to another. This chapter gives you only an overview of the topic and enough of the commands to get you started.

Although there is much more to know, you already have come a long way toward using the Internet services to get the information you need. This chapter showed you two different commands to make a direct connection, rlogin and telnet, which enables you to use a remote computer as though you were using a terminal directly connected to it. You also have learned how to use telnet and ftp to move files and programs from those computers to your own account.

The three most valuable services on Internet are e-mail, telnet, and ftp. You have completed your introduction to all three. Think of yourself as a child who has just learned to read. Next, you should practice these new skills while exploring the topics that interest you.

You now have the information you need to become an Internet explorer. Travel the Internet highways and see what you can discover for yourself. As you gain competency using these commands, you will learn of more useful information, and in time you will take for granted your access to the immense store of information available to you from all over the world.

CHAPTER 4

Using Netnews

If you have used the forums on CompuServe, or similar confer-
ence systems on other on-line services, then you have an idea of
what Netnews is. It is a way in which you can connect with many
people all over the world who are interested in the same topics
that you are. It's also a way to get quick—though not necessarily
correct— answers to questions that might start out, "Say, does
anybody know... ."

Netnews can be entertaining, enlightening, infuriating, and an
incredible time sink. It tends to be addictive. You have been
warned. :-)

Incidentally, that :-) is a smiley, which will be explained later in
this chapter.

Other things you will learn in this chapter are:

→ The difference between Netnews and the Internet

→ What newsgroups are available and how they are organized

→ Which postings are appropriate or inappropriate

→ The kinds of software you can use to read news

→ Basic information on how to read and post news

Understanding Netnews

"Usenet is like a herd of performing elephants with diarrhea—massive, difficult to redirect, awe-inspiring, entertaining, and a source of mind-boggling amounts of excrement when you least expect it."

—Gene Spafford, 1992

Netnews is somewhat different from CompuServe's forums. For one thing, it is much, much bigger. Internet old-timers (from, say, five years ago) talk about the old days, when a person could read everything that had been posted to Netnews the previous day and still have time to get work done that morning.

For another, though Netnews's size is limited in somewhat the same way that CompuServe forums are, forums tend to be limited by the number of messages in them; Netnews messages don't pile up indefinitely, they *expire* after a particular time period, set by the system administrator at the Netnews site.

Netnews includes both work-related information, such as discussing PCs, Macintoshes, and Unix, and other information, such as discussing television, science fiction, and sports. Although one could argue that people using the Net for research purposes should be discussing their work, not what was on "Star Trek" last night, in practice people would discuss it anyway. Therefore the people who designed the software felt it was better to accept that people would do a certain amount of non-work–related discussion, and at least put it in an area by itself where it would not interfere with other discussions.

Usenet and How It Is Different from the Internet

Computers that provide Netnews do so through special software that lets them exchange postings, or articles, with other computers, similar to the way that e-mail is exchanged. The network of computers that exchange Netnews is sometimes called *Usenet*.

Although many machines on the Usenet also are on the Internet, the two terms are not synonymous. A computer does not need to be on the Internet to exchange Netnews with other machines, in the same way that a computer does not need to be on the Internet to exchange electronic mail. Similarly, not all machines on the Internet provide Netnews to their customers, though many do.

In addition, not all machines on the Usenet are Unix systems, though they frequently are. But even a Macintosh or a PC can run software that enables it to exchange Netnews with other machines, though the details of how to set that up yourself are beyond the scope of this book.

GETTING THE TERMINOLGY RIGHT

It is important to make the distinction between Usenet and Internet, if only so Internet gurus do not make fun of you for making the mistake. Because of the possibility for confusion, this book will describe the news network in terms of Netnews instead of using the term Usenet.

Differentiation between Netnews and E-mail

E-mail and Netnews often are exchanged over the same communications channels at the same time, but they are different in a couple of crucial ways. One is that e-mail is private, going only to specified recipients, while Netnews is public, going to anyone who subscribes to a newsgroup. Another is that Netnews expires, or is automatically deleted, after a specified time period, while e-mail stays in a recipient's account indefinitely, unless deleted by a systems administrator.

As described in Chapter 3, some mailing lists normally transmitted through e-mail also are available through Netnews. You can choose to read these messages through whichever method is more convenient to you. E-mail's feature of staying indefinitely can be either an advantage—if, for example, you do not have the opportunity to read the messages frequently—or a disadvantage—if, for example, your mailbox fills up with unwanted messages.

Similarly, Netnews software provides features such as *killing*, or automatically deleting from your view, groups of messages unread, such as all messages with a particular subject line or by a particular person. If you know that you will not want to read all of the messages on a particular mailing list, Netnews software will let you ignore those messages more efficiently.

How Big Is Netnews?

By whatever method you use to measure, Netnews is huge. At the time this book was written, for example, there were more than 3,000 newsgroups, or specific topic areas. Netnews transmits more than 10 megabytes of data per day. (Only a few years ago, Netnews transmitted less than 1 megabyte of data per day.)

Traditionally, like e-mail, Netnews was exchanged between machines using uucp, or Unix-to-Unix Copy. These days, many machines use nntp, or Net News Transfer Protocol. This improved software, coupled with the speedier telecommunications links that many Internet machines have, means that an article you post to Netnews may appear in minutes, when it used to take days.

PROVIDING NETNEWS GROUPS

What is most amazing about Netnews is that it is not controlled by any person or group. Any site systems administrator can determine which groups, if any, the site chooses to offer—with the proviso that a site that is downstream from another site, from which it gets its Netnews, cannot offer a Netnews group that the upstream site does not offer. In other words, the WELL, for example, can provide only the Netnews groups that one of the sites feeding it provides.

How Netnews Groups are Created

New Netnews groups are generally voted upon by all the existing Netnews users, though in practice only a small fraction of Netnews users vote on any proposed Netnews group. Before the vote, the proposed Netnews group is discussed by interested parties. The initial proposal is called an RFD, or *request for discussion*; after it appears that discussion has reached its end, the call for an RFV, or *request for vote*, is made. Certain rules are specified, such as the number of votes to be received for the vote to be considered valid, or the percentage of yes votes that must be received for the Netnews group to pass.

Once the vote is held, if the proposed Netnews group passes, then a create group command begins to traverse the Usenet, and users can begin to post messages to that Netnews group.

Similarly, votes are occasionally held to remove a Netnews group, usually one that has outlived its usefulness or been replaced by a number of more specific groups.

The Newsgroup Hierarchy

In the same way that machines on the Internet are organized into a hierarchy, Netnews groups are similarly organized. The first level of the hierarchy is shown in table 4.1.

Category	Meaning
alt	**Alternative**, referring not to the subject of the newsgroup, but to the alternative Netnews group hierarchy. Netnews groups in this hierarchy are not held to as rigorous an approval standard; in fact, anybody can create an `alt` newsgroup.

Table 4.1:

Netnews Group Hierarchy

continues

Table 4.1:
continued

Category	Meaning
bionet	**Biology network.** Netnews groups in this area all cover biological technology.
bitnet	Newsgroups that also are mailing lists on the **"Because It's There"** (or **"Because It's Time,"** depending on which legend you prefer) network, primarily composed of educational institutions.
biz	**Business**-related Netnews groups, such as some commercial announcements and services.
clari	News articles and features found in "print" newspapers and organized according to subject.
comp	**Computer**-related Netnews groups.
de	**Deutsche.** Netnews groups in German.
fj	**Japan.** Netnews groups in Japanese.
fr	**France.** Netnews groups in French.
ieee	Netnews groups concerning work by the **Institute of Electrical and Electronic Engineers**.
misc	**Miscellaneous** topics.
news	Netnews groups covering **Netnews** itself, including its administration and management.
rec	Netnews groups covering **recreational** topics.
sci	Netnews groups covering **scientific** topics.
soc	**Social** topics, covered by Netnews groups such as cultural groups.
talk	Netnews groups covering controversial, much **talked-about** topics, such as gun control and abortion.

Category	Meaning
us	Netnews groups that cover the **United States**.
vmsnet	Netnews groups covering Digital Equipment Corp.'s DEC **VAX minicomputer** (which sometimes runs the **VMS operating system**, which is where the name comes from).

In addition, individual machines may have their own Netnews groups, specifically for Netnews readers on that machine. Both Netcom and the WELL, for example, offer Netnews groups for their users.

NEWS GROUPS FOR SPECIFIC LOCALES

TIP

Individual states and geographic areas also have Netnews groups devoted to them, depending on the needs and desires of users in those areas. For example, there are both ba—Northern California Bay Area—and ca—the state of California—Netnews groups, covering topics such as housing, jobs, and current events. Sometimes the groups are available outside their geographic area, which can be useful if you are trying to keep up-to-date with a remote area.

Within each main hierarchy, a number of Netnews groups can be set up, which can themselves have their own hierarchies. For example, within the comp area are separate hierarchies for operating systems and data communications, each with a number of groups within them. The hierarchies can go three or four deep.

When Netnews was first set up, the hierarchies were much shallower; for example, nearly all the topics in rec, soc, and talk were covered in the net hierarchy. (Of course, in those days, the amount of information transmitted in Netnews each day was much smaller.) Old-timers sometimes refer to that period as "the old days, when the Net was flat," meaning a flat hierarchy.

Individual Netnews Groups

Each Netnews group has its own personality, conventions, and history, and the same person might post very differently in two different Netnews groups.

Some Netnews groups are *moderated*, for example, which means that, like some mailing lists, they are governed by a moderator to whom such postings are sent, and who decides whether a particular submission is posted. The advantage of such Netnews groups is that they often offer a higher signal-to-noise or light-to-heat ratio—meaning the proportion of valuable information in that newsgroup tends to be higher than in comparable, unmoderated Netnews groups. The disadvantage is that response is slower, and it can be difficult to hold unpopular positions or speak out against the moderator.

Finding Accessible Netnews Groups

On some machines with Netnews, a list of all available newsgroups is stored in the file /usr/lib/news/active. To read this file, you type:

```
more /usr/lib/news/active
```

Then press Enter. The more item is a paging program that will stop after each screenful of text and wait for you to type a character before it continues.

In addition, another file, usually less complete but somewhat more useful, is available that includes one-line descriptions of the Netnews groups and the purpose for each. However, if the Netnews group creator was not conscientious, this description may be missing. This file may be available as /usr/lib/news/ newsgroups. To read this file, type the following:

```
more /usr/lib/news/newsgroups
```

Press Enter. On Netcom, for example, the contents of this file are a 65-page description of available Netnews groups.

CONTROVERSIAL NETNEWS GROUPS EXIST

In case you did not know, Netnews groups are sometimes created on controversial topics and in controversial topic areas, ranging from homosexuality or drugs to gun control or the best kind of editor program. Consider this a warning so that you will not be surprised later.

You do not need to read these articles if you do not want to; you can unsubscribe from a Netnews group on abortion, for example, if you do not approve of abortion. It is unlikely that you will be able to convince the Netnews hierarchy to stop carrying a particular group, nor that you could convince gay Netnews users to change their orientation, so it is pointless to try to get a properly chartered Netnews group removed or to fill up a Netnews group with flames. "Live and let live" is a longtime Netnews motto.

Exploring Different Kinds of Netnews Software

To read Netnews, you generally will have to use some kind of software on your Internet system specifically designed for reading and posting to Netnews.

READING NEWS WITHOUT SOFTWARE

Specifically designed software is not absolutely required for you to read Netnews. You could, for example, find the names of the files in which the articles for each Netnews group are stored, and then read through them with an editor or a Unix display command such as `more`, but this would be a great deal of work and not very efficient.

Some of the most popular Netnews reading programs are:

➡ **nn.** This stands for No News and is intended for users who expect that they will skip over the majority of Netnews messages in a newsgroup. It requires vt100 terminal emulation; nn shows you a list, a screenful at a time, of the Netnews messages in each Netnews group to which you are subscribed, and you select the messages you wish to read. nn also groups together messages with the same heading so that you can see connections more easily. (For example, if you have used CompuServe's Forums, they also sort messages into threads with the same headers.)

➡ **rn.** This stands for Read News. It is one of the classics in Netnews reading software—which means it is widely available but was designed for the days when the Net was flat and consisted of only 1M of "traffic" a day. Consequently, it can be laborious to use, especially if you are subscribed to many Netnews groups but do not expect to read most of the postings. It also can be cryptic.

➡ **tin.** This program uses *threading*, which means that Netnews articles with the same subject are grouped together; it is intended to be easy to use, and offers a menu-based interface. Unfortunately, at the time this book was written, tin was not widely available.

➡ **trn.** This stands for Threaded Read News. It essentially is a version of rn that, like tin and nn, groups Netnews articles into threads based on their subject lines. It is becoming more widely available. Some systems that supported rn have renamed trn to rn, so this threaded version of rn runs instead of the original program.

➡ **readnews.** This program is one of the really old Netnews readers, and it generally has been superseded by one of the others. On the other hand, it also does not require that you have a particular form of terminal emulation, so if you are running old communications software that does not support vt100 emulation, you may find it useful. Also, readnews stores articles differently than many of the other news readers do. Therefore, supporting this program and another (like `rn`) requires that two copies of each article be stored on the system. For this reason it is rarely available anymore.

→ **vnews.** This is a full-screen version of `readnews`.

→ **emacs.** As with reading e-mail, `emacs`, which technically is an editor but contains a plethora of other features, has two ways to read Netnews: `gnus` and `gnews`, of which `gnus` is the most common. This Netnews reader is quite powerful; you can program it to show you all the articles written by a given person, delete unread (as far as you are concerned; they remain for other users) all the articles written by a given person or on a given subject, delete all those articles except those written by particular people, and so on. However, being `emacs`, it is quite cryptic and can place quite a load on your Internet system.

All of these news readers do the same kind of thing: they share common terminology. Each of the programs mentioned in the preceding list look at the database of news articles and let you use tools to choose what you want to read. The choices you make are stored in a special file in your directory and this file is used each time you use the news reader. Your choices only affect what you see and never change the big database of articles that everyone reads from. For example, news readers refer to deleting or killing a subject or newsgroup, but that doesn't mean those articles are truly deleted. It only means you will not see them.

One of the things every news reader does is keep track of which groups you like to read. These are referred to as the groups that you are *subscribed* to. All other groups are referred to as *unsubscribed.*

Another thing all news readers do is organize articles. Generally they are grouped by topic as people follow up or add an article to an ongoing discussion. This process, as touched on in the preceding list, is referred to as *threading* the articles. Each discussion in a group can be thought of as one thread.

SETTING Ann EXAMPLE

It is beyond the scope of this book to give a complete tutorial on each of these Netnews readers—indeed, entire books could be written about each of them. Because nn is fairly easy to use and more widely available than tin, the examples in this chapter will use nn.

Using the .newsrc File

Netnews reading programs keep track of the Netnews groups to which you have subscribed, and the articles that you have read, with a file called .newsrc. If you have never read Netnews on your existing Internet system, you will not have this file yet. A very small section of one is shown in figure 4.1.

There are several things to notice about entries in this file. First, note that each entry has, after the name of the Netnews group, either a : or an !. The : indicates that the owner of this file currently is subscribed to that Netnews group, while the ! indicates that the owner of this file is not subscribed to that Netnews group.

Next, the entries in the .newsrc file have numbers after them. These numbers indicate which articles on that Internet system the owner of this file has processed—either by reading, deleting, or skipping over them. (Note that even an unsubscribed Netnews group has numbers after it; that simply means that Netnews considers those articles processed although they were not actually read. They may have simply timed out.)

```
rec.music.afro-latin! 1-607
rec.music.beatles! 1-11138
rec.music.bluenote! 1-11353
rec.music.cd! 1-20312
rec.music.christian! 1-4541
rec.music.classical! 1-24697
rec.music.country.western! 1-3562
rec.music.dementia! 1-2848
rec.music.dylan! 1-5321
rec.music.early! 1-1128
rec.music.folk: 1-22875
rec.music.funky! 1-2139
rec.music.gaffa! 1-16343
rec.music.gdead! 1-45735
rec.music.industrial: 1-26127
rec.music.makers! 1-19416
rec.music.misc: 1-100055
rec.music.newage! 1-6496
rec.music.reviews! 1-274
rec.music.synth! 1-26331
rec.music.video: 1-3167
```

Figure 4.1:
A `.newsrc` file.

NUMBERING THE `.newsrc` ARTICLES

TIP

The number associated with each article is different on every system with Netnews; the articles are numbered based on factors such as when they arrive on the system and how long the system has been receiving that particular Netnews group. Referring to a particular article by its number not only is useless to people outside your own system, but will mark you as a neophyte, or a "clueless newbie."

Because nearly all Netnews readers use this `.newsrc` file, reading Netnews for a while with one program and then another may affect this file. This may be an advantage or a disadvantage. You might try a new Netnews reading program that you don't understand, for example. If it automatically marks all the new articles as being processed, it will be difficult for you to use your customary Netnews reading program to read those articles. On the other hand, if you would like to read some Netnews groups with one Netnews reading program and other Netnews groups with another one, then the single `.newsrc` file lets you do that.

The first time you read Netnews, your Netnews reading program may automatically subscribe you to every Netnews group on your Internet machine—which could amount to more than 2,000 groups—and you will have to unsubscribe from each of them manually. However, if you know how to use an editor on your Internet system, you can edit the `.newsrc` file and do a global replace on each line from : (or subscribed) to ! (or unsubscribed).

Alternatively, you can download the `.newsrc` file from the Internet system to your PC or Macintosh, perform the global replacement there, and then upload it back to the Internet system.

If you are using a new Netnews reading program or performing other Netnews experiments, make a copy of your `.newsrc` file on your Internet system.

DON'T UNSUBSCRIBE FROM EVERYTHING

If you unsubscribe to everything from the very beginning, it can be difficult to get into nn in the first place; if there are no new articles to read, the software will reply:

```
No News (is good news)
```

You will then exit from the program. So be sure you are subscribed to at least a couple of Netnews groups, such as the ones dedicated to your Internet system. You might want to start with news.announce.newusers.

Taking Caution Before You Post Articles

Before you post an article to Netnews, your Netnews posting software may ask you something like:

```
This message may go to hundreds of Usenet sites around
the world. Are you sure you want to do this?
```

This is not hyperbole. Posting articles to Netnews should be taken very seriously, even more so as the Internet becomes larger. It is easy to create a reputation on-line that can come back to haunt you. If you make an ass of yourself on the Net, don't be surprised if dozens of people write you letters telling you just what a jerk you are.

Copies of Netnews articles have recently become available on CD-ROM. It may be an urban legend at this point, but it is rumored that some companies, before hiring new employees, will check out their Netnews postings on this CD to see what sort of things they say on-line and whether this is the sort of person they want to hire. Whether true or not, it isn't debatable that the technology now exists to do this.

In addition, remember that for every person who contributes to a Netnews group, there are numbers of *lurkers*, or people who read Netnews articles without taking the risk of posting anything themselves. So even if it seems like you know most of the people in a Netnews group and feel comfortable telling them details of your life or confidential data about your job, remember that many other people may be seeing these articles as well.

Some of these lurkers may also send you e-mail about your articles or the views you express in them. In some cases, you may not object to this; in others, this e-mail might be annoying, and could become persistent or abusive.

Opinions vary on how to deal with such messages, but generally people will agree that, if you have asked the person to stop sending you e-mail and they persist, then you should consider informing their systems administrator or postmaster.

Reading and Posting to Netnews Using nn

The next part of this chapter discusses the mechanics of reading and posting articles using the nn Netnews reading program. This chapter will cover only the basic features of nn; if you wish to learn more, check to see whether your Internet system offers a manual with more information.

Also, you can get more information about nn by typing the following:

```
man nn
```

You then press Enter.

Commands in nn are case-sensitive—q and Q mean two different things, for example. Be sure you are using the appropriate case when entering a command.

In addition, check your Internet system to see what other Netnews reading programs might be available; if tin is available, for example, you may wish to check that out. Information on these programs, if present on your system, should also be available using man.

To run nn, type nn and press Enter. To exit nn, type Q.

Subscribing and Unsubscribing to Netnews Groups

To either subscribe or unsubscribe to a Netnews group, type U while in that Netnews group. The software then will respond as shown in figure 4.2.

The U command (note the uppercase) is a toggle, meaning that if you are unsubscribed to the Netnews group, it will ask you if you want to subscribe; if you are subscribed to the Netnews group, it will ask you if you want to unsubscribe. To change your subscription status to that Netnews group, type y.

Going to Other Netnews Groups

Using nn generally reports the Netnews groups to you in alphabetical order, but you might want to see a Netnews group at other times—if you want to go back to check something, for example, or if there is something you want to look at quickly. In addition, if there are no new articles in the Netnews group, or if you are not subscribed to it, then nn will not show the group to you; you will have to go to it manually to see it at all.

```
Newsgroup: news.announce.newusersArticles: 15 of 148/42 UNSUB READ *NO*UPDATE*

a.Jonathan Kamens 732   Changes to List of Periodic Informational Postings
b.Jonathan Kamen  1271  List of Periodic Informational Postings, Part 1/6
c.Jonathan Kamen  1250  >List of Periodic Informational Postings, Part 2/6
d.Jonathan Kamen  1177  >List of Periodic Informational Postings, Part 3/6
e.Jonathan Kamen  1149  >List of Periodic Informational Postings, Part 4/6
f.Jonathan Kamen  1307  >List of Periodic Informational Postings, Part 5/6
g.Jonathan Kamen  1338  >List of Periodic Informational Postings, Part 6/6
h.Jonathan Kamens 783   How to become a USENET site
i.Jonathan Kamens 276   Introduction to the *.answers newsgroups
j.Stephanie Silva 978   Publicly Accessible Mailing Lists, Part 1/5
k.Stephanie Silv  1356  >Publicly Accessible Mailing Lists, Part 2/5
l.Stephanie Silv  1171  >Publicly Accessible Mailing Lists, Part 3/5
m.Stephanie Silv  1269  >Publicly Accessible Mailing Lists, Part 4/5
n.Stephanie Silv  1345  >Publicly Accessible Mailing Lists, Part 5/5
o.Ron Dippold      698  Usenet Newsgroup Creation Companion

Already unsubscribed.  Resubscribe to news.announce.newusers ?



ALT-F10  HELP  | ANSI-BBS | FDX |  4800 N81 | LOG CLOSED | PRT OFF | CR  |  CR
```

Figure 4.2:

Subscribing or unsubscribing to a Netnews group using nn.

The command for going to a Netnews group is as follows:

```
G Netnews group name
```

In this case Netnews group name is, of course, the name of the Netnews group you want to see. Then press Enter.

Now, what if you do not know the exact name of the Netnews group? The G command (note the upper case) can find all the Netnews groups that contain a particular key phrase and asks you if you want to go to that Netnews group. If you want to look at Netnews groups for the Macintosh, for example, but are not sure which Netnews group might be the best one, you could type the following:

```
G mac
```

You then press Enter, and nn offers each of the Netnews groups with mac in the name until you select one. It will ask if you want to go to any of the groups containing the string mac, even if you are currently unsubscribed to them.

After you select a group, nn responds by asking which articles you want to see, as shown in figure 4.3.

```
Newsgroup: news.announce.newusers        Articles: 15 of 148/42 READ *NO*UPDATE*

a.Jonathan Kamens 732   Changes to List of Periodic Informational Postings
b.Jonathan Kamen 1271   List of Periodic Informational Postings, Part 1/6
c.Jonathan Kamen 1250   >List of Periodic Informational Postings, Part 2/6
d.Jonathan Kamen 1177   >List of Periodic Informational Postings, Part 3/6
e.Jonathan Kamen 1149   >List of Periodic Informational Postings, Part 4/6
f.Jonathan Kamen 1307   >List of Periodic Informational Postings, Part 5/6
g.Jonathan Kamen 1338   >List of Periodic Informational Postings, Part 6/6
h.Jonathan Kamens 783   How to become a USENET site
i.Jonathan Kamens 276   Introduction to the *.answers newsgroups
j.Stephanie Silva 978   Publicly Accessible Mailing Lists, Part 1/5
k.Stephanie Silv 1356   >Publicly Accessible Mailing Lists, Part 2/5
l.Stephanie Silv 1171   >Publicly Accessible Mailing Lists, Part 3/5
m.Stephanie Silv 1269   >Publicly Accessible Mailing Lists, Part 4/5
n.Stephanie Silv 1345   >Publicly Accessible Mailing Lists, Part 5/5
o.Ron Dippold     698   Usenet Newsgroup Creation Companion

Goto comp.sys.mac.advocacy ?


ALT-F10  HELP | ANSI-BBS | FDX | 4800 N81 | LOG CLOSED | PRT OFF | CR. | CR
```

Figure 4.3:

Selecting which articles to see in a Netnews group.

Your most likely options are a, e, and u (but don't be afraid to try other options). The a option means "Show me all the articles that are available in this Netnews group on this machine, no matter how old they are and whether I already have read them." The u option means, "Show me all the articles that are available in this Netnews group on this machine that I have not already read."

HOW TO REVIEW YOUR NEWS LIST

If you go through a Netnews group and then realize you want to take another look at it before exiting nn, note that nn does not revise the .newsrc file until you exit nn. Instead, if you use the G command to go to a Netnews group after going through it already, and select u, you still will see all of the articles that were new to you in this nn session.

The other likely choice is e, which lets you select a keyword for nn to look for in the Sender: or Subject: fields. If you want to see all the articles in comp.sys.mac about the Quadra, for example, you type the following:

    e

Then when nn displays an =, you type:

    quadra

Similarly, if you remember that somebody named John posted something interesting, you type **e john** when nn displays an =. The e option shows you all the articles with the keyword, regardless of whether you have read them.

Also note that the e command is not case-sensitive—that is, it will look for John, john, and every other combination when you type john.

Reading Articles

When you access a Netnews group in nn, whether you did so manually or not, you are shown a list of available articles, as in figure 4.4.

You should take note of several things about this screen. First, see that nn displays just enough articles to fill your screen, and then pauses.

Next, notice that both the name of the person posting the article and the subject of the article are given. Sometimes you will want to read an article specifically because you know the person posting it; sometimes you will avoid articles written by particular people.

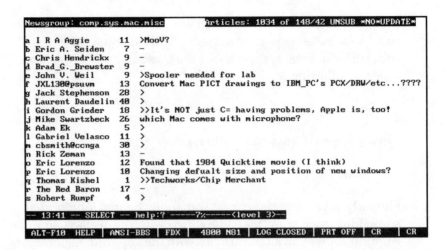

```
Newsgroup: comp.sys.mac.misc        Articles: 1034 of 148/42 UNSUB *NO*UPDATE*
a I R A Aggie        11  >MooU?
b Eric A. Seiden      7  -
c Chris Hendrickx     9  -
d Brad_G._Brewster    9  -
e John V. Weil        9  >Spooler needed for lab
f JXL130@psuvm       13  Convert Mac PICT drawings to IBM_PC's PCX/DRW/etc...????
g Jack Stephenson    28  >
h Laurent Daudelin   40  >
i Gordon Grieder     18  >>It's NOT just C= having problems, Apple is, too!
j Mike Swartzbeck    26  which Mac comes with microphone?
k Adam Ek             5  >
l Gabriel Velasco    11  >
m cbsmith@ccnga      30  >
n Rick Zeman         13  -
o Eric Lorenzo       12  Found that 1984 Quicktime movie (I think)
p Eric Lorenzo       10  Changing defualt size and position of new windows?
q Thomas Kishel       1  >>Techworks/Chip Merchant
r The Red Baron      17  -
s Robert Rumpf        4  >
-- 13:41 -- SELECT -- help:? -----7%-----<level 3>--
ALT-F10  HELP | ANSI-BBS | FDX |  4800 N81 | LOG CLOSED | PRT OFF | CR  |  CR
```

Figure 4.4:

Available articles in a Netnews group in nn.

In addition, you can see that sometimes the name is not really a proper name, but a nickname. Some Internet systems enable you to do this, while others require you to use your proper name.

WHAT DOES > MEAN?

Some subjects have the > character in front of them, or even multiple > characters. Those characters mean that the articles are part of a series—responses to other articles.

Sometimes you will see a subject with a - character in front of it. Remember that articles do not necessarily reach your machine in the same order. The - indicates that the article is the first in the thread, even though other articles with the same subject have reached your Internet machine before it.

To tell nn that you want to read a particular article, type the letter that appears in the first column of that line. When you do that, nn highlights the line, as shown in figure 4.5.

To select an article to read, press the letter it is listed by. You can change your mind by pressing the letter again.

```
Newsgroup: news.announce.newusers        Articles: 15 of 173/48 READ *NO*UPDATE*
a.Jonathan Kamens 732    Changes to List of Periodic Informational Postings
b.Jonathan Kamen 1271    List of Periodic Informational Postings, Part 1/6
c.Jonathan Kamen 1250    >List of Periodic Informational Postings, Part 2/6
d.Jonathan Kamen 1177    >List of Periodic Informational Postings, Part 3/6
e.Jonathan Kamen 1149    >List of Periodic Informational Postings, Part 4/6
f.Jonathan Kamen 1307    >List of Periodic Informational Postings, Part 5/6
g.Jonathan Kamen 1338    >List of Periodic Informational Postings, Part 6/6
h.Jonathan Kamens 783    How to become a USENET site
i Jonathan Kamens 276    Introduction to the *.answers newsgroups
j.Stephanie Silva 978    Publicly Accessible Mailing Lists, Part 1/5
k.Stephanie Silv 1356    >Publicly Accessible Mailing Lists, Part 2/5
l.Stephanie Silv 1171    >Publicly Accessible Mailing Lists, Part 3/5
m.Stephanie Silv 1269    >Publicly Accessible Mailing Lists, Part 4/5
n.Stephanie Silv 1345    >Publicly Accessible Mailing Lists, Part 5/5
o.Ron Dippold      698   Usenet Newsgroup Creation Companion

-- 13:43 -- SELECT -- help:? -----All-----<level 2>--



ALT-F10  HELP | ANSI-BBS | FDX |  4800 N81 | LOG CLOSED | PRT OFF | CR  |  CR
```

Figure 4.5:

Selecting an article
to read in nn.

When you have selected all the articles on that screen that you
wish to read, press the spacebar. This tells nn that you want to
move on to the next screenful of available articles. (Note that you
do not press the spacebar after you select each letter.)

When you reach the end of the list of available articles, nn ends
the list with a line like that shown in figure 4.6.

```
Newsgroup: news.announce.newusers        Articles: 15 of 173/48 READ *NO*UPDATE*
a.Jonathan Kamens 732    Changes to List of Periodic Informational Postings
b.Jonathan Kamen 1271    List of Periodic Informational Postings, Part 1/6
c.Jonathan Kamen 1250    >List of Periodic Informational Postings, Part 2/6
d.Jonathan Kamen 1177    >List of Periodic Informational Postings, Part 3/6
e.Jonathan Kamen 1149    >List of Periodic Informational Postings, Part 4/6
f.Jonathan Kamen 1307    >List of Periodic Informational Postings, Part 5/6
g.Jonathan Kamen 1338    >List of Periodic Informational Postings, Part 6/6
h.Jonathan Kamens 783    How to become a USENET site
i Jonathan Kamens 276    Introduction to the *.answers newsgroups
j.Stephanie Silva 978    Publicly Accessible Mailing Lists, Part 1/5
k.Stephanie Silv 1356    >Publicly Accessible Mailing Lists, Part 2/5
l.Stephanie Silv 1171    >Publicly Accessible Mailing Lists, Part 3/5
m.Stephanie Silv 1269    >Publicly Accessible Mailing Lists, Part 4/5
n.Stephanie Silv 1345    >Publicly Accessible Mailing Lists, Part 5/5
o.Ron Dippold      698   Usenet Newsgroup Creation Companion

-- 13:43 -- SELECT -- help:? -----All-----<level 2>--



ALT-F10  HELP | ANSI-BBS | FDX |  4800 N81 | LOG CLOSED | PRT OFF | CR  |  CR
```

Figure 4.6:

Reaching the end
of the available
articles in nn.

Note that the line has the word All in it, indicating that these are
all the articles.

At this point, if you press the spacebar, nn will show you, one at a time, each of the articles you have selected. If you have not selected any articles, then nn will take you to the next Netnews group.

SAVING ARTICLES FOR LATER

What if you do not have time to read every newsgroup you would like, and you would like to at least look at what is new in other groups? Type N and press Enter to tell nn that you want to go to the next Netnews group, instead of reading the present articles. They will be there for you the next time you run nn— unless you wait long enough that your Internet system expires them before you return. If you have selected articles, they will still be selected when you return.

If you have selected an article, it will appear on your screen, as shown in figure 4.7.

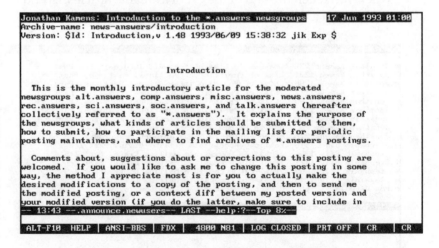

Figure 4.7:

An example of nn displaying an article.

Note, again, that nn shows you just one screenful of the article, and pauses until you tell it that you are ready for the next screenful. Note, too, that the last line of the screen shows how many unread articles there are, and what percentage of the articles you have read. If there are no more Netnews articles in this group after the one you are reading, the bottom line of the screen will say LAST.

When you have finished reading this screen of the article, press the spacebar and nn will show you the next screen. If this is the last screen of the article, then nn will take you to the next article. If this is the last screen of the last article, then pressing the spacebar will take you to the next Netnews group.

Clearing Your Screen

Sooner or later you will get a mail message notice or line noise written to your screen while you are reading news. This messes up the display and is confusing if you don't know how to clear the garbage off your screen. The nn command to redraw the screen is ^L.

Getting Back to the Menu While Reading News

The equal sign command (=) is also very useful. If you use it while reading an article, it will enable you to return to the menu of articles in that particular group.

Summarizing Useful Commands

If you know only the following commands, you know enough to enjoy reading Netnews. Start with this list and learn others from within the program using ? or by reading the man pages.

General commands, for use at any time:

?   Context-sensitive help; this will list a page of useful commands

U   Subscribe and unsubscribe; this has a toggle (off/on) effect

Q   Quit and exit the program

G   Go to the specified newsgroup

Message commands, for use while reading messages:

p	Previous article
n	Next article
D	Decrypt a rot13 file
s	Save
r	Reply
f	Follow up
=	Return to menu
^L	Clear screen

Interpreting a Netnews Article

The first few times you read Netnews, the articles may seem arcane. They can be full of > characters, odd indentations, acronyms, and seemingly meaningless combinations of symbols. But they actually do make sense after a while.

First, the > characters and indentations indicate quotes from another person's article in the thread. Newsnet posters do this because the articles may not arrive on different machines in the same order, and an article without such quotes might not make sense. The quotes also enable the Netnews poster to provide context for his or her replies.

The way nn indicates this quoted material varies depending on the Netnews software that the person writing the message used. Most commonly, the software uses > for each level of quotes. This means that, for example, if Person C is replying to Person B who is replying to Person A, Person A's postings will have >> in front of them, while Person B's postings will have > in front of them.

RECOGNIZING DIFFERENT QUOTES

Some Netnews posting software uses tab characters to indent quoted material. On the other hand, some Netnews posting software puts tabs in front of the replies to the quoted material. Some other Netnews posting programs use the quoted poster's ID in front of each line. So, for example, if Rick's article is being quoted, it will look like this:

```
Rick> quoted material

Rick> quoted material

Rick> quoted material

New material appears this way
```

Now, about those acronyms. Many Netnews posters like to use acronyms in their articles. Some of these date from on-line uses such as CompuServe's CB Simulator, and other real-time uses, in which people tried to reduce the number of characters they needed to type. Some of the most common are shown in table 4.2.

Acronym	Meaning
OTOH	On the other hand
IOW	In other words
IMHO	In my humble opinion
IMNSHO	In my not-so-humble opinion
RTFM	Read the "fine" (or other adjective) manual
FYI	For your information
BTW	By the way
SO	Significant other

Table 4.2

Common Acronyms in Netnews

Last are those combinations of characters. They started out with
:-). If you look at it sideways, you can see that it looks like a
smiling face. (Some people eliminate the nose and use :).)
Netnews posters use them to indicate irony, jokes, or sarcasm,
none of which translate well in the on-line medium. (Serious
addicts use them even in handwritten correspondence.)

Then, Netnews posters began varying the basic :-). One early
variation was :-(, for unhappiness or bad news; another was ;-),
for a wink. Since then, dozens have been developed and are used
occasionally, though in practice Netnews posters generally stick
with just a couple of the basics. See Appendix D, "The Unofficial
Smiley Dictionary," for a plethora of smiles that you can amuse
yourself and others with.

In groups like rec.humor you will run across postings which are
encrypted because they are offensive to some readers. This
encryption is called *rot13*. To read postings that look like they
were composed of random characters, type D. The article will
reappear unencrypted.

Saving an Article

While reading a Netnews article, you may find that you would like
to save a copy of it. To save a copy of a Netnews article on your
Internet system within nn, type **s**; nn responds with a screen like
that shown in figure 4.8.

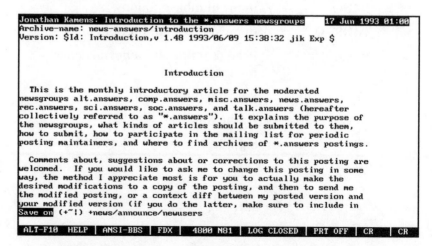

Figure 4.8:

Saving an article.

Note, first, that you do not need to read through the entire Netnews article before saving it—you can save it at any time.

Also, nn automatically specifies a file name in which to store the Netnews article; press Enter and nn will save the Netnews article in that file name. Or, by using the Backspace key and the rest of your keyboard, you can type in a different name—deleting the default file name if you wish. When you have finished typing the file name with which you would like the Netnews article to be saved, press Enter.

If the file does not exist, nn will ask you if you want it to create a file by that name, as shown on the bottom line in figure 4.9.

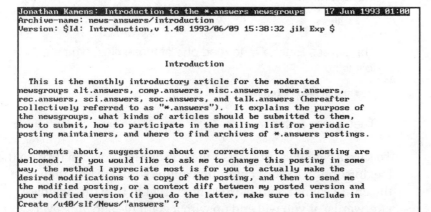

Figure 4.9:

Creating a file for a Netnews article (see bottom line).

You can either type **y** to create the file, or **n** to not create the file, in which case the Netnews article will not be saved and you will need to start the process over if you still wish to save a copy of the Netnews article. If you type something other than n or y, nn will continue to ask you to give one of those responses.

If the file already exists—perhaps you are keeping a record of a number of Netnews articles on a particular topic—then this Netnews article will be *appended*, or saved, onto the end of the existing file.

Now, any time you wish to read that Netnews article again, you can read it just as you would any other file on your Internet system.

A QUICK WAY TO FIND FILES

Many Internet systems are set up such that Netnews articles and files are in a different directory than your base, or home, directory. That is, if you are logged in to your Internet account and try to read the file, you will need to remember to specify that the file is in the News directory. To see a list of all the file names in which you have stored Netnews articles, for example, type the following:

```
ls News
```

Then press Enter. Or, to read one of those files, type the following:

```
more News/filename
```

Then press Enter.

To save a Netnews article as a file on your PC, you can turn on the logging option in your communications software and then read the entire Netnews article. (Do not forget to turn off logging afterwards, or you will end up with a giant file showing everything you do in your Internet session.) You could also save it as a file on your Internet system, then download it as a file to your PC.

Killing a Thread

Sometimes a Netnews discussion in which you have no interest will start, and you would like to be able to skip over those messages. Fortunately, nn offers you a way to do this, called "killing" the message thread.

To do this, when you are in a Netnews group, type K. Note the use of the uppercase. When you type this, nn will respond as shown in figure 4.10.

```
Newsgroup: comp.sys.mac.misc          Articles: 1034 of 173/48 UNSUB *NO*UPDATE*
a cbsmith@ccnga      ?  Where does the IIvx fit in nowadays?
b Chris Robson      21  -
c Chris Hendrickx   30  -
d Steve Fouts       33  -
e Tricia Cox        35  >
f Paul Donahue      19  >>
g W. Rowe           18  >
h Steve Fouts       34  -
i Mr N Plastique     8  >>>
j cbsmith@ccnga     51  -
k Brian Kendig      41  >>
l Paul Donahue      19  >>
m Paul Donahue      18  >>>
n cbsmith@ccnga     78  >>>
o cbsmith@ccnga     24  >>>>
p cbsmith@ccnga     51  -
q Paul Donahue      11  >>>
r Chris Barrus      25  >>>
s Steve Fouts       34  -

AUTO (k)ill or (s)elect (CR => Kill subject 30 days)

ALT-F10  HELP | ANSI-BBS | FDX | 4800 N81 | LOG CLOSED | PRT OFF | CR | CR
```

Figure 4.10:

Killing a thread in nn.

As you can see, nn offers three choices: killing the thread permanently; killing the thread for a month, which is the default; or
specifying a number of criteria by which to kill the thread. You
might want to kill the thread for a month, for example, if you are
too busy to read it now, but may be interested in reading other
articles on that topic when you are less busy. More frequently,
you kill a thread for a month in hopes that a busy discussion will
subside by then. To kill the thread for a month, just press Enter.

To kill the thread permanently, type **k**. Then, nn will ask you to
indicate which topic you want killed. Type the letter that appears
in the left column of one of the articles under the subject header
you want killed. You do not have to type the letter of the first such
article; for example, if articles a-1 are on the topic you want killed,
you can type any of the letters between a and 1 to kill the thread.

EFFECTS OF KILLING A THREAD

TIP

Note that you are killing the thread for only you; it will still be
available to other users on your Internet machine and on other
machines. However, if you have killed the thread, the killing still
will take effect even if you specifically request to see articles on
that topic using the G newsgroup command and e.

After you have killed the thread, though, you still may occasionally see articles with that subject header. Why? It is because nn only kills articles in a thread—that is, articles that were in a string of replies to each other. If somebody has posted an article with that same subject line, for example, but it is not in response to one of the other articles with that subject header, then nn will not kill it.

To kill a thread through other criteria, type **s** at the K prompt. At that point, K will enable you to kill a thread based either on its subject—for example, all articles containing a certain phrase, whether or not there are other words in the article's subject header as well—or the name of the person who posted it.

You then can choose whether to kill Netnews articles meeting that criterion in all Netnews groups or only in the Netnews group you are in. Next, you choose the time period for which to kill Netnews articles meeting those criteria, with the default being 30 days.

Responding to Netnews

At some point while reading Netnews, you will want to respond to something you have read. There are two ways you can do this. First, you can reply to the original Netnews poster in e-mail. In Netnews lingo this is referred to as *replying*. Second, you can reply to the Netnews poster with an article of your own. This is called *following up*.

Replying

To reply to an article in nn, select it and begin to read it, then type **r**. You do not need to read the entire article to reply to it. When you do this, nn will reply with the following:

```
Include copy of article?
```

In other words, nn is offering to include a copy of the Netnews article to which you are replying so that you can quote the Netnews article in yours.

In general, it is less important to quote a person's article when you are following up to it than when you are replying to it. You can assume that a person is going to remember his own article. Nevertheless, it still can be a good idea to remind the person of the parts of the article to which you are replying.

To include a copy of the Netnews article to which you are replying, type **y** and press Enter. If you do not want to include a copy of the article, type **n** and press Enter. Most of the time you will want to include the original article and then delete unnecessary parts of it.

Then, nn will put you into the editor (probably emacs or VI) in use at your Internet system so that you can type in your response. The mechanics of how to use the editing program is beyond the scope of this book; this program could be any of a number of editors, and the best source of information on this is your Internet systems provider.

When you have finished typing your response, exit the editor. When you have done that, nn will ask if you wish to mail the message or post (send) the article, depending on whether you have indicated that you wanted to reply or follow-up, as follows:

```
a)bort e)dit h)old m)ail r)eedit s)end v)iew w)rite

Action: (post article)
```

As you can see, sending (posting) the message or article is the default; you can just press Enter to select it. Then nn returns you to the article to which you just responded.

Following Up

To follow up to an article, select it and begin to reedit, then type the following:

```
f
```

Note the lowercase. This command will work exactly like the r (or reply) command except that your message will go only to the author of the original message through e-mail.

Posting an Article

To post an article that is not in response to an existing one, you use a separate program called nnpost. To use it, type **nnpost** and press Enter.

Both nnpost and postnews will ask what newsgroups to post to, what the subject is, for keywords, for a summary, and for a distribution. An example follows:

```
Newsgroups: soc.singles
Subject: dating
Keywords: money, places
Summary: need ideas for cheap things to do on dates
Distribution: (default 'world')
```

You will need to list the newsgroups you want to post to *exactly* as they should be spelled. If you list more than one group, readers can view it from any of those groups. Once a reader views or kills it from any of the groups where it appears, it will be gone from sight in all groups where it is listed. So if you post to both misc.legal and alt.child-support, it will only appear to readers of both groups once.

Putting more than one newsgroup on a subject line (separated by spaces) is called cross-posting. It is considered bad manners to post the same article twice to different groups by using nnpost twice with only one group listed each time.

When nnpost asks you for a subject, give a short, three or four word summary of what your posting will be about.

When nnpost asks you for keywords, you can list any significant words someone may want to search for to find your type of article. You do not have to list any keywords, but many users find it useful if you do.

The summary line allows you to expand on the subject with just a few more words. You should still try to keep this short.

The distribution question is asked so you can specify how widely your article will be distributed. The default will be as wide as possible. In the preceding example, this is the entire world. You might limit that by giving another possible answer. Your message will only be seen in North America if you answer na, or in the United States if you answer usa. Usually you type local or your two letter post office state abbreviation to limit distribution to the local organization or to a state.

As with replying to or following up another Netnews article, nnpost puts you into your Internet system's default editor to actually create the message. When you have finished doing this and have exited the editor, nnpost will display the same message as you would see if you were following up an existing article:

```
a)bort e)dit h)old m)ail r)eedit s)end v)iew w)rite

Action:
```

To post (send) the article, press Enter or type **s**. To edit the article again, type **e**. To abort the whole process, type **a**.

How to Get Additional Help

The command to get help in nn is ?. You can type it almost anywhere to view a screen of the most common commands and explanations of what those commands do. The help command itself is context-sensitive, which means that the list of commands you see depends on what you were doing when you called for help. Only those commands that will work at the screen where you are currently will appear.

Although nn is a very complex program, it isn't necessary to learn all about it. This section has mentioned only a very few of the available commands. Generally, if you find yourself thinking there must be a way to do something, there probably is. When you have mastered the commands in this chapter and want to learn to use nn more efficiently, use the man nn command to see more. This opens the nn online "manual"—over 70 screen pages of information dedicated to nn alone.

Creating a .signature File

As you read articles, you will see that many of them include information at the end, such as the poster's name, address, e-mail address, and a pithy quote. No, the poster does not type this for each article. Instead, the Netnews posting software automatically appends to each article the information located in a special file called a .signature file. This is pronounced "dot signature."

To create a .signature file, use your Internet system's editor to create a file named .signature and then type into that file the information that you would like appended to each of your postings. By convention, .signature files should be limited to four lines or less. In fact, some Netnews posting software will not allow you to post a message with a longer .signature file, or may only append the first three lines.

If you read Netnews any time at all, though, you soon will learn that many people do not follow this convention. Instead, they may include elaborate graphical creations, long quotes, and so on. This becomes very tiresome to people reading the articles. It is the equivalent to long, elaborate messages on answering machines, which you must sit through before being able to hear the beep.

Also, remember that a .signature file that fits very well in rec.arts.jokes may not be appropriate in comp.lang.c. Again using the answering machine analogy, it is as though you had a silly or dirty message on your answering machine, and then your boss called.

IT HELPS TO TEST YOURSELF

When you first start posting articles to Netnews, you may be a little unsure of yourself and feel a bit of performance anxiety at the notion of talking to a million people at once. Yet, in the same way that we get tired of nervous speakers tapping the mike asking, "Is this thing on?" Netnews users get tired of reading messages that go, "Ignore this, please—this is a test." A number of Netnews groups are set up specifically for such tests, whether it is for a new user to test Netnews software or for a network administrator to check on the path that Netnews takes between machines.

If you are concerned that your article will not make it out to the world, or that you are making some heinous mistake, send it to one of the test groups instead. Both the Well and Netcom feature test groups, for example. There is also a `misc.test` worldwide test group if you can't find a local one.

Having a Problem?

After posting articles to Netnews, you likely will run into someone whose articles you do not like, or who takes an issue with your articles.

In general, the best way to react with such a person is to ignore him. Remember that Netnews has no central authority; there is no Netnews Police who will come and take Netnews access away from your tormentor.

However, in some cases it may be appropriate to take your problem to a higher authority. Examples of such cases are:

→ The person begins threatening you

→ The person contacts you at home or work through surface mail or telephone, or even by trying to meet you in person, against your wishes

→ The person posts confidential information about you to Netnews, such as your credit card numbers

→ The person begins to contact your superiors at work or the system administrators of your Internet account

The person best suited to deal with such problems is the system administrator or postmaster of your Internet system. Do not attempt to solve the problem yourself through guerrilla tactics such as sending enormous files of data to the person; this is liable to get *you* in trouble as well, and will seriously diminish your credibility in the matter.

On the other hand, do not expect your system administrator to become upset over complaints such as "He flamed me!" or "She called me a name!" It is sad, but true, that at this point many of the users of Netnews are college students, and sometimes their tactics for dealing with people with whom they disagree make that obvious.

For the most part, people using Internet news are intelligent and honest. They will not want to be publicly embarrassed any more than you would.

Summary

This chapter has described the way that Netnews works and suggested some programs you can use that enable you to read Netnews. You now also know how to use the basic commands of one of these programs, nn.

Moreover, by now you know how to use the basic Internet tools of e-mail, telnet, ftp, and Netnews. Now that you know how to get and transmit information, the final chapter will explain to you how to *locate* information.

CHAPTER 5

Finding Information on the Internet

One of the biggest problems with using the Internet is finding things. All sorts of wonderful things are all over the Internet, but unless you know where they are, they do not do you any good.

However, the tools that help you use the Internet are some of the fastest-growing areas in Internet development. Areas of development such as ftp, e-mail, and telnet are settled; helping users like you find information is now the most exciting new Internet frontier.

This chapter will discuss some of the most common tools for finding information and locations of information on the Internet, including:

➡ whois

➡ finger

➡ uu commands

→ gopher

→ archie

→ WAIS

→ World-Wide Web

→ Other useful resources from the Net

Starting the Search

If you were going on an automobile trip and wanted to get information about your destination and route, you would have a number of options. Depending on how much effort you wanted to put in, you could:

→ Ask your friends and relatives if any of them have been there, and what experiences they had

→ Read articles in your local newspaper, the newspapers from your destination, and newspapers from the areas in-between

→ Read articles in travel magazines and regional magazines about the area you are visiting

→ Call the Chambers of Commerce for your destination and the areas in-between

→ Call travel associations, such as the AAA, and ask them for advice and information

→ Visit the library and look for books

→ Buy books

→ Read maps

Well, if you are going exploring around the Internet, it will help if you do the Internet equivalents. You would examine your resource options in order to answer a rather broad question: *Who knows what about which parts of the Internet, and how do you access that information?*

Asking Questions

The simplest way to find information is to ask someone who knows, though that might not seem as glamorous a way as using some sort of exotic tool. The easiest way to find out someone's e-mail address, for example, is not to use a directory or send out a program to find it, but to ask them.

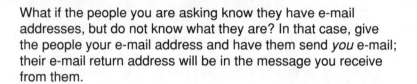

AND IF THAT FAILS...

What if the people you are asking know they have e-mail addresses, but do not know what they are? In that case, give the people your e-mail address and have them send *you* e-mail; their e-mail return address will be in the message you receive from them.

It is better to ask a specific person, if you know one who knows the information and if the information you are asking for is not too complex, than to put out a general request to the world. For example, a number of the Frequently Asked Questions (FAQs) for the various Netnews groups specifically request that you not post Netnews articles in those groups along the lines of, "Can anybody please help me find... ." Some of these FAQs themselves include information on where you can find things; remember to look in appropriate Netnews groups, including ones such as news.answers, before posting such articles.

Using whois

The function whois is, more or less, "white pages" for all the users at an organization or an educational institution. An overall white pages for the Internet does not exist at this point, but a number of organizations do offer this service.

To get a list of whois servers, type:

```
ftp sipb.mit.edu
```

Then press Enter. Log in as **anonymous** with the password being your Internet address; you type:

```
cd pub/whois
```

Press Enter and type:

```
get whois-servers.list
```

Press Enter. The list of whois servers is included in Appendix E.

To use whois on a particular server, type:

```
whois -h servername searchname
```

Then press Enter.In this command line *servername* is the name of the whois server you are checking, and *searchname* is the name for which you are searching.

USING VARIOUS whois FORMS

Note that, if you are searching for a multiple-word name—such as Sharon Fisher—you generally enclose the name in quotes to tell whois that the name is a single unit: "Sharon Fisher". However, some other whois servers are set up differently, and may expect the name in the form of *firstname.lastname*, *lastname,firstname*, *firstname lastname*, or *firstname_lastname*. If "*firstname lastname*" does not appear to work, try one of these other forms.

If you omit the servername, then whois will automatically check a database called the *InterNIC Registration Services Host*. This database used to accept unlimited registrations, but policy on that is changing; "ordinary people" (users with no special credentials or qualifying classification) may be purged from that database soon.

Figure 5.1 contains an example of searching for an entry for President Clinton.

```
{Netcom:8} whois clinton
Clinton, Crush (CC217)          SPX30@PENTAGON-AMSNET.ARMY.MIL
                                   (512) 221-3903 (DSN) 471-3903
Clinton, Doug (DC206)           dec@ALEX.COM              +44 81
566 2307
Clinton, Glenn (GC170)          PMEL4-2@AG-LOGDIS1-AFLC.AF.MIL
(DSN) 488-6717
Clinton, Glenn E. (GEC7)     pmel48-4@LOGDIS1.AG.AFLC.AF.MIL   DSN:
226-3857
Clinton, Glenn E. (GEC29)    gclinton@ODS-HOST1.ARMY.MIL
                                   011-966-3-011-966-3-4404
Clinton, Marshall P. (MPC)   clinton@VAX.LIBRARY.UTORONTO.CA
        (416) 978-7649
Clinton, Perry J. (PJC29)    aetv-pa-ab-adm@WUERZBURG-
EMH1.ARMY.MIL350-6463
Clinton, Reginald [TSgt.] (RC428) LGPD@AVIANO.AF.MIL
                   39-0434-667014 (DSN) 632-7014 (ETS) 632-
7381
Clinton, Terry (TC158)          TERRY@AFSC-BMO.AF.MIL
                                   (714) 382-2353 (DSN) 876-2353


To single out one record, look it up with "!xxx", where xxx is
the
handle, shown in parenthesis following the name, which comes
 first.

Please note that all INTERNET Domain, IP Network Number, and ASN
records are now kept in the new Internet Registry,
RS.INTERNIC.NET.
This whois server only contains DOD Information.
```

Figure 5.1:
A whois search for President Clinton.

As you can see, the whois information also includes the sentence `To single out one record, look it up with "!xxx", where xxx is the handle, shown in parenthesis following the name, which comes first`. This means that you can get more complete information—such as an address—about any of those users listed by typing:

whois !handle.

You then press Enter.

However, your Internet system may reply with a message such as:

```
Unmatched ".
```

This is because the ! is used as a special command character with some Unix systems. If you are trying to get specific information about a handle and get an error message, type a backslash (\) in front of the exclamation point, as follows:

```
whois \!handle
```

Then press Enter. The \ indicates to the operating system on your Internet system that the ! should be used as a piece of text rather than as a command.

TIP

INTERNET ETIQUETTE

It is considered bad manners to use the whois servers for large-scale searches or in an attempt to obtain large quantities of the database for your own use. It is especially bad form to do so for commercial purposes—for example, obtaining many government users to create a list for junk mail.

Using finger

The Unix program called finger gives you information about other Internet users. To use it, type **finger** followed by the user's user name and address (@*machinename.organization*), as shown in figure 5.2.

Typing finger *name@machinename.organization* gives you the information about all the users with *name* in their *username* at the *machinename.organization* site.

```
Terminal type is vt100
{Netcom:1} finger sharon@netcom.com
[netcom.com]
Login name: sharon                     In real life: Sharon Fisher
Directory: /u41/sharon                 Shell: /bin/csh
Last login Fri Jul  2 15:20 on ttyp7 from netcom2
Mail last read Wed Jul 14 00:15:15 1993
No Plan.
{Netcom:2}
```

| ALT-F10 | HELP | ANSI-BBS | FDX | 4800 N81 | LOG CLOSED | PRT OFF | CR | CR |

Figure 5.2:

Using finger.

If you are sure that you know the exact user name of the person, you can type:

> finger -m *username@machinename.organization*

When you press Enter, finger will you give you information about that specific user name. The finger -m command tends to search faster, and of course you are then presented with the information only for that one particular user.

Note that finger can provide information such as the user's name, when he last logged on (or whether they are logged on at the time), how long his session has been idle (for example, perhaps he went to lunch but left his terminal logged in), and when he last received e-mail. Then finger displays a file in that user's account called .plan. (For example, you can use finger to check for someone being on-line and not idle, so that you can initiate a real-time chat with him.)

TIP

If you are using finger to get a user on the same system you are on, you can just type **finger *username*** or **finger -m *username***—that is, you do not need to type the machine name.

FINGER TIP

The `finger` command can be used without specifying a user name to see who is logged into a computer. Use the finger command in the form **finger *@machinename.organization*** to see a list of all the people currently using that machine.

How much information you get depends on the Internet site you are using `finger` to reach, and on the specific user. For example, some sites consider "incoming `finger`," or the ability of an outside user to get information about users on the system, to be a security risk—intruders can use `finger` to find out when users are on-line and when they are not, and can use that information to determine when to break into the system.

In addition, in the Morris worm incident of 1988, one of the methods that Morris used to break into remote computers was by exploiting a well-known but unrepaired bug in the `finger` program.

THE ROBERT MORRIS WORM INCIDENT

On Nov. 2-3, 1988, 6,000 computers on the Internet—many of them vital to university research, national defense, and government operations—were brought to their knees by a virus.

The rogue program attacked gateway (not the brand name) computers that controlled access to other computers and spread faster than programmers could act to stop it. By the time it was stopped, the virus had caused untold millions of dollars in damage due to lost time, productivity, and human resources used to stem the crisis.

Eventually the person who wrote and implemented the virus, Robert Tappan Morris, was apprehended. Morris was a graduate student in computer science at Cornell University, and had intended the virus to be harmless. A mistake in writing the program, however, caused the virus to run out of control. Morris was tried for computer fraud, convicted, and sentenced to three years probation and a $10,000 fine. See the "Security" section in Chapter 1.

Consequently, some organizations limit the information that their `finger` programs provide.

Adding Information to Your `finger` with `.plan` or `.project`

It is possible for you to make additional information about yourself available to those you `finger` by using a `.plan` or a `.project` file. Look at the following example of a typical `finger`:

```
figure klw.finger
```

The project is a single line of information. It might be a short job description, witty comment, or a philosophical comment on Life. To make a project, save only a single line of text called `.project` with your favorite editor. Put this file in your home directory and change the permissions on the file so it can be read by all.

In this "figure" (see the command line preceding), the `.plan` is a cartoon. These `.plans` are more commonly used to list upcoming vacation plans, schedules of meetings, or deadlines for upcoming projects. This file can be any length but you will probably want to keep it fairly short so all of your finger information will fit on only one screen.

Users can choose whether to create a `.plan` file, and what information to put in such a file about themselves for other people to read. Some users make very personal, long, or elaborate `.plan` files, while others have basic files or no `.plan` files at all.

You can create your file either on your Internet system, using an editor program available there, or on your PC, and then upload it to the Internet system.

PLAN YOUR .plan

Remember that for people on other machines to be able to read your .plan file, you need to create that file with the proper permissions, as described in Chapter 1. The file will need to be world-readable, or else people trying to finger you will be told that you do not have a .plan file.

Advantages and disadvantages exist in creating a .plan file, the same way that there are advantages and disadvantages to being listed in a telephone directory or getting on a mailing list. The advantage is that it is easier for people to find you. However, that is also the biggest disadvantage—some people who will be able to find you are people whom you would just as soon avoid.

Keep in mind that it is also possible that, if you are using Internet as part of your job, your company may have its own policies on what can be said in a .plan or .project file.

Using finger for Other Remote Machine Information

You also can use finger @machinename.organization to find out all the users currently logged in on machinename, as shown in figure 5.3.

In addition, some sites use finger to disseminate short pieces of information. You can finger that user and site, and get a message.

Using the uu Commands

You can get information about machines connected to the Internet by uucp—that is, both Internet machines and machines not directly connected—with a number of commands that begin with uu. (Incidently, uucp stands for *Unix-to-Unix copy*.) These commands use data in a file called uumap. For the uu commands to work on a particular site, that site needs to have an entry in the uumap file. Not all the uu commands are available on all systems.

```
{Netcom:2} finger @netcom2.netcom.com
[netcom2]
Login     Name           TTY Idle  When   Where
forte    Forte           p0   8 Fri 14:04 NETCOM-
al5.netco
prufrock Thomas A. Faulhaber  p1    Fri 08:04 NETCOM-
pa1.netco
logan    Wolverine       p2    Fri 13:59 NETCOM-
pa1.netco
lyle     Lyle Fong       p3    Fri 13:23 NETCOM-
al3.netco
bobzub   Bob Alexander   p4    Fri 12:59 NETCOM-
al3.netco
cattrone Paul Cattrone   p5    Fri 14:16 NETCOM-
al5.netco
dserrano Danny Serrano   p6    Fri 14:08 NETCOM-
al3.netco
mcgowan  Bonnie McGowan  p7    Fri 14:05 NETCOM-
al5.netco
jwsb     Justin Broughton p8  3 Fri 14:03 NETCOM-
al5.netco
glr      Gary Reisch     p9    Fri 14:14 NETCOM-
la1.netco
c3       C-Cube Microsystems *pa   Fri 12:11 NETCOM-
sj4.netco
erc      Eric Smith      pb   2 Fri 11:02 NETCOM-
al5.netco
slf      Sharon Fisher   pc    Fri 14:17 NETCOM-
al3.netco
lukec    Luke Chastain   pd   1 Fri 10:45 NETCOM-
al5.netco
netmail  E-Mail support Accou *pe   Fri 07:52 admin
.
.
.
```

Figure 5.3:

Using finger on a machine.

uuhosts

The uuhosts command gives you information about a particular site, such as who is responsible for it and what sorts of uucp connections it has with other sites. This information can be useful if you are trying to send e-mail to a uucp site and you want to figure out which other sites it calls most frequently.

uuwhere

Although uuhosts still is available on some systems, on others it has been replaced by uuwhere. The uuwhere *machinename.organization* command displays the path between the machine you are currently using and the *machinename.organization* site. From the Well, for example, any other machine on the Internet is one "hop" away. So uuwhere netcom produces the following:

    netcom.com

However, with a machine that does not have a direct Internet connection, uuwhere shows how to get to that machine through other ones. For example, uuwhere thelema produces the following:

    decwrl.dec.com!thelema

This shows that messages addressed to users on the machine thelema can be routed through decwrl.dec.com—for example, *username*%thelema@decwrl.dec.com.

uuwho

The uuwho command shows the entry in the uumaps file for a particular machine. Information in such entries includes a contact name and number, a description of the machine, and the other machines it exchanges information with. For example, uuwho well produces figure 5.4. On the other hand, uuwho netcom produces figure 5.5.

```
{Netcom:12} uuwho well
System name:    well
System type:    Sun SPARCstation 2; SunOS 4.1.2
Organization:   Whole Earth 'Lectronic Link
Contact person: Bill Wisner
Email Address:  well!wisner
Telephone:      +1 415 332 4335
Postal Address: 65M Gate Five Road, Sausalito, CA 94965
Long/Lat:       37 51 15 N / 122 29 15 W
Remarks:        also nkosi.well.sf.ca.us [129.132.30.4]       on
the Internet
Remarks:        The WELL is a commercial computer conferencing
system with over
Remarks:        200 public conferences available only to
customers.  Private
Remarks:        conferences are       available at no extra
charge.  The WELL   offers
Remarks:        access to e-mail, USENET and the Internet.
Rates are $15/month   +
Remarks:        $2/hour.  We can also be reached through the
CompuServe   dialup
Remarks:        network        for an extra $4/hour from almost any
city in the continental
Remarks:        United States. Additional charges apply for
international connections.
Remarks:        Call us or send mail to info@well.sf.ca.us
for more information.
Remarks:        On the phone: +1 415 332 6106 (300-2400bps)
Remarks:        On the Internet: well.sf.ca.us [192.132.30.2]
News links:     moon pacbell.com uunet
Author & date:  well!wisner (Bill Wisner); Mon Apr 19 14:13:42
PDT 1993

#

well   .well.sf.ca.us
well=  well.sf.ca.us
well   dollar(DAILY/5), fico(DAILY/7),    forever(DEAD),
hake(DAILY),
       halfdome(DIRECT+FAST), helix(WEEKLY/4),    kerner(DAILY/5),
       moon(DIRECT+FAST), pixpc(WEEKLY/6), satlink(WEEKLY/7),
       sense8(DAILY/3), taz(WEEKLY/5), twics(DAILY),
ugbn(DAILY/8),
       unicom(DAILY/2), uunet(DEDICATED), wet(HOURLY), z-
code(DIRECT+FAST)
```

Figure 5.4:

The **uuwho** entry
for the WELL.

```
Netcom:13} uuwho netcom
System name:    netcom,      .netcom.com, netcom.com,
netcom.netcom.com
System type:    Sun 4/670, SunOS
Organization:   Netcom - Online     Communication Services
Contact person: Robert Hood
Email Address:  netcom!postmaster
Telephone:      +1 408 554-UNIX
Postal Address: 4000 Moorpark Avenue - Suite 209, San Jose, CA,
95117
Long/Lat:       37 10 01 N / 121 53 19 W
Remarks:        UNIX/Communications Services: Info: +1 408 241-
9760
Remarks:        90 Telebit V.32/V.42   login: guest
Remarks:        IP (telnet): 192.100.81.100
Remarks:        Local access SF, Berkeley, San Jose, Santa Cruz,
Palo Alto, Pleasanton
Remarks:        Shell accounts,        UUCP/USENET feeds, Internet
connections
News links:     netcomsv
Author & date:  netcom!postmaster (Robert Hood); Tue Aug 18
11:13:02 PDT 1992

#

netcom =        netcom.com
netcom =        netcom.netcom.com
netcom.netcom.com(LOCAL)
netcomnetcomsv(LOCAL)
```

Figure 5.5:

The uuwho entry for Netcom.

Using gopher

The program known as gopher is very easy-to-use; intended for novices, it helps retrieve information from machines on the Internet. It uses a standard, menu-based interface, called a gopher client, and runs over ftp, hiding much of ftp's complication from you. A *standard interface* means that the way you use the program looks the same to you, regardless of where the information is that you are retrieving.

This client communicates with gopher servers, or programs located on various other systems on the Internet that actually provide the information. For example, gopher uses some of the systems described later in this chapter, such as WAIS and WWW.

GOPHER? WHY SUCH A NAME?

The gopher program was originated at the University of Minnesota. Apparently, gopher's programmers were considering a triangular analogy when they named it: A gopher (large rodent) tunnels underground and out of sight, much as gopher's interface structure does; a "gofer" in your office efficiently expedites numerous tasks, again, like gopher; and the official mascot of the University of Minnesota is... the Golden Gopher.

It is also possible to download a gopher program (that runs on your PC) that automatically logs on to gopher systems and retrieves information. However, such programs generally require more sophisticated communications software than a standard dial-up communications package, and so are beyond the scope of this book.

OVERLY POPULAR gopherS

Be aware that some gopher servers are very popular, and that the owners of those systems have had to restrict their availability—for example, limiting the number of people who can log on at one time. If a gopher server suggests "Try again later," then do just that.

Using gopher Directly

You can use gopher by running a gopher client on the Internet system you are using, and calling another system that has a gopher server running. For example, if you type:

```
gopher gopher.well.sf.ca.us
```

and press Enter, you will get a screen like that shown in figure 5.6

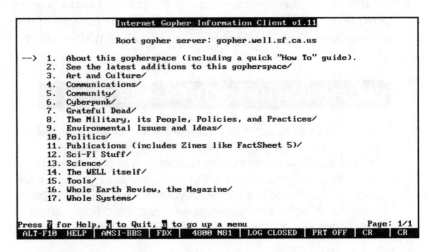

As you can see, gopher starts out by giving you a menu of choices
with a simple interface. To select an item, such as Cyberpunk, you
can either use the cursor keys to move the arrow to the appropriate number (6), or just type **6**. Then, press Enter, and the gopher
program shows you the next screen (see fig. 5.7).

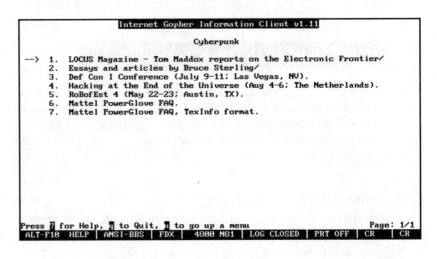

Figure 5.7:

The Cyberpunk
menu on the
WELL's gopher
server.

WHAT'S A CYBERPUNK?

Mondo 2000, a computer technology-culturist-futurist-political commentary-entertainment magazine, takes a stab at defining *cyberpunk*: 1. a late 20th Century techno-revolutionary, or someone who poses as such; 2. a hard-boiled hacker with anarchist inclinations; 3. a computer geek who likes (rock band) Ministry; 4. as seen in *TIME* magazine, a member of a counter-cultural "movement" of the same name, characterized by a combination of technological savvy with a rebellious lifestyle.

Bruce Sterling, a noted author in the science fiction and cyberpunk area, offers a number of his writings available through the WELL's gopher. To see a list of what is available, type **2** and press Enter, and you see yet another menu. The first one is called "Read this First!" and describes Bruce's copyright policies. The last screen of it is shown in figure 5.8.

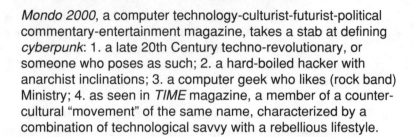

Figure 5.8:
The Bruce Sterling menu on the WELL's gopher server.

TIP

gopher **VERSATILITY**

Notice that gopher enables you to save this information in a file, print it, or e-mail it to somebody. If you type **m**, the gopher server gives you a field in which you can type an e-mail address—your own or somebody else's—and the gopher server sends the file to them.

To exit the gopher server, after you are done with the Bruce Sterling document, type **q**. The gopher server will ask you if you really want to quit, and if you type **y**, it will end the program.

Accessing gopher **from a Server**

If your Internet system does not offer a gopher client, you can use the telnet command to transfer to a gopher server site and use the information there.

For example, you can type:

```
telnet consultant.micro.umn.edu
```

You then press Enter and log in as gopher. The server will ask you what kind of terminal you have, and after you enter that information, you will get the screen shown in figure 5.9.

```
           Internet Gopher+ Information Client v1.2beta5

                    Root gopher server: gopher2.tc.umn.edu

  -->  1.  Information About Gopher/
       2.  Computer Information/
       3.  Internet file server (ftp) sites/
       4.  Fun & Games/
       5.  Libraries/
       6.  Mailing Lists/
       7.  News/
       8.  Other Gopher and Information Servers/
       9.  Phone Books/
      10.  Search Gopher Titles at the University of Minnesota <?>
      11.  Search lots of places at the U of M <?>
      12.  UofM Campus Information/




Press ? for Help, q to Quit, u to go up a menu              Page: 1/1
ALT-F10  HELP  | ANSI-BBS | FDX  |  4800 N81 | LOG CLOSED | PRT OFF | CR  |  CR
```

Figure 5.9:

The opening screen at the University of Minnesota gopher server.

Note that this gopher server specializes in information about gopher itself. You can type **1**, and then press Enter, for example, to get more information about gopher.

To move back up through the hierarchy of menus, type **u**.

Exploring gopher Servers

In the United States alone, there are more than 400 gopher servers—26 screens full if you access the on-line list—at the time this book was written. To get the current list, connect to the umn.edu gopher server, as shown in the previous section, and then select 8 for more information about servers, as shown in figure 5.10.

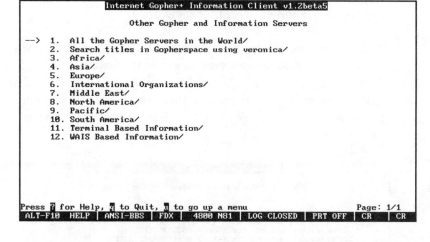

Figure 5.10:
More sources for gophers.

Then select 8 again, for North America, then 3, for the U.S. You can either read the whole list or pick one state at a time.

In addition, new gopher servers and new information to existing ones are being added all the time. To get the most up-to-date list of gopher servers:

➡ Read the alt.gopher and comp.infosystems. gopher Netnews groups. The alt.gopher Netnews group is geared more toward users, while the comp.infosystems Netnews group is aimed toward organizations that are providing gopher services.

→ Connect periodically to the `consultant.micro.umn.edu` server and see what is new.

→ Subscribe to the `gopher` mailing list by sending e-mail to `gopher-news-request@boombox.micro.umn.edu`.

Using `veronica`

The program called `veronica`, which stands for Very Easy Rodent-Oriented Net-wide Index to Computerized Archives, is designed to help you find `gopher` repositories that contain the information you are looking for. (It is the equivalent to the `archie` program, described later in this chapter, which finds files in `ftp` archives. Archie and Veronica are a couple of teenagers in a comic book. Get it?) You give `veronica` a keyword, and it searches the `gopher` repositories it knows of for that keyword.

To run `veronica`, use the `telnet` command to access the University of Minnesota `gopher` server as shown in the previous section "Accessing `gopher` from a Server." Then, type **8** (followed by Enter) to get more information about `gopher` servers, and **2** (followed by Enter) for `veronica`. You will get a screen like that shown in figure 5.11.

```
┌──────────────────────────────────────────────────────────────────┐
│           Internet Gopher+ Information Client v1.2beta5            │
│                                                                    │
│             Search titles in Gopherspace using veronica            │
│                                                                    │
│      1.                                                         .   │
│      2.  FAQ:  Frequently-Asked Questions about veronica  (1993/06/24). │
│      3.  How to compose  veronica queries (NEW June 24) READ ME!!. │
│      4.  Search gopherspace for GOPHER DIRECTORIES  (U. Pisa) <?>   │
│      5.  Search gopherspace for GOPHER DIRECTORIES  (UNR) <?>       │
│ --> 6.  Search gopherspace using veronica at UNR <?>               │
│      7.  Search gopherspace using veronica at University of Pisa <?> │
│                                                                    │
│                                                                    │
│                                                                    │
│                                                                    │
│                                                                    │
│                                                                    │
│ Press ? for Help, q to Quit, u to go up a menu         Page: 1/1   │
│ ALT-F10  HELP │ ANSI-BBS │ FDX │ 4800 N81 │ LOG CLOSED │ PRT OFF │ CR │ CR │
└──────────────────────────────────────────────────────────────────┘
```

Figure 5.11:

The `veronica` screen.

Note that this screen also enables you to read information about how to use veronica effectively. You do not want to ask a question that is too vague, for example, or you might get thousands of responses. Similarly, you do not want to ask a question that is too specific, or you might get no responses.

Say that you want to see what information there is on animation. Type **6** and then press Enter to indicate that you want to formulate a veronica query. veronica will then ask you for your search criteria, and you type **animation** and press Enter (see fig. 5.12).

```
   Internet Gopher+ Information Client v1.2beta5

       Search titles in Gopherspace using veronica

   1.                                                    .
   2.  FAQ: Frequently-Asked Questions about veronica  (1993/06/24).
   3.  How to compose  veronica queries (NEW June 24) READ ME!!.
   4.  Search gopherspace for GOPHER DIRECTORIES  (U. Pisa) <?>
lqqqqqqqqqqqqqqqqqqqSearch gopherspace using veronica at UNRqqqqqqqqqqqqqqqqqqqk
x                                                                              x
x Words to search for  animation                                              x
x                                                                              x
x                           [Cancel ^G] [Accept - Enter]                      x
x                                                                              x
mqqqqqqqqqqqqqqqqqqqqqqqqqqqqqqqqqqqqqqqqqqqqqqqqqqqqqqqqqqqqqqqqqqqqqqqqqqqqqqqj




Press ? for Help, ? to Quit, ? to go up a menu              Page: 1/1
ALT-F10  HELP | ANSI-BBS | .FDX |  4800 N81 | LOG CLOSED | PRT OFF | CR  |  CR
```

Figure 5.12:
Making a veronica query.

In a remarkably short period of time, you get your response, as shown in figure 5.13.

Note that it is 11 screens long! To get any of these files, all you need to do is type the number associated with the file and press Enter. gopher automatically will fetch those files for you, without your knowledge of where they are or how to retrieve them.

As you can see, gopher and veronica are very powerful tools and examples of the new ways that the Internet is beginning to be used.

```
╔══════════════════════════════════════════════════════════════════╗
│         Internet Gopher+ Information Client v1.2beta5              │
│                                                                    │
│          Search gopherspace using veronica at UNR: animation       │
│  --> 1.   animation-faq.                                           │
│      2.   3DLIB15.ZIP - 3D animation library for TP6, TPW & utilities. │
│      3.   3DLIB14.ZIP - 3D animation library for TP6, TPW & utilities. │
│      4.   CoVis for animation.                                     │
│      5.   Computer and Information Sciences 262. Computer Animation. S. │
│      6.   Computer Animation.                                      │
│      7.   Stop-Frame Animation.                                    │
│      8.   ANIMATION & CARTOONS/                                    │
│      9.   faq.animation.                                           │
│     10.   Making an animation.                                     │
│     11.   Making an animation.                                     │
│     12.   4(5) Sep92 "Human Animation, Computers, Dance" (Calvert)  SFU-CSS. │
│     13.   X window fonts converter to Rayshade 3.0 polygons, Rayshade animat../ │
│     14.   agocg-animation/                                         │
│     15.      Re: Computer Animation.                               │
│     16.      Re: Computer Animation.                               │
│     17.      AART: Animation Video Request. Berlin..               │
│     18.   Japanese Animation Infospace Project/                    │
│                                                                    │
│  Press ? for Help, q to Quit, u to go up a menu      Page: 1/11    │
│  ALT-F10  HELP │ ANSI-BBS │ FDX │ 4800 N81 │ LOG CLOSED │ PRT OFF │ CR  │ CR │
╚══════════════════════════════════════════════════════════════════╝
```

Figure 5.13:

The results of a veronica query.

Using `archie`

The program called `archie` (derived from *archive*), as mentioned
in the previous section, looks for code on the Internet in `ftp`
repositories. Like `gopher`, you can run `archie` either as a program
on your Internet site, if it is available there, or by using `telnet` to
go to an `archie` server, and doing a search there.

Running `archie` Directly

To run `archie` on your local Internet machine, type **archie** followed by the name of the program for which you are searching.
You can either type it in exactly, or, by typing **archie -s** instead,
you can type in part of the name and `archie` will look for programs containing that name.

For example, there is a public-domain encryption package called
Pretty Good Privacy (PGP) that enables you to encode your data
so that no one can read it without knowing the key. Typing **archie
pgp** from Netcom would yield a screen full of directories. You
could then use this information to log in to those systems using
`ftp`, and then see what material is in those directories. Or, if you
want to do a more elaborate search, type **archie -s pgp**, which will
do a search for all programs that have `pgp` in their names.

Running archie from a Server

If the Internet system you are using does not support a direct archie client, then, as with gopher, you need to use telnet to connect to an archie server elsewhere. There is one at archie.ans.net, for example. To use it, type:

telnet archie.ans.net

You then log in as:

archie

At this point you see the screen shown in figure 5.14.

```
login: archie
*─────────────────────────────────────────────────────────*
! ── The default search method is set to "exact".          !
! ── Type "help set search" for more details.              !
!                                                          !
! Other Servers:                                           !
!   archie.unl.edu          129.93.1.14                    !
!   archie.sura.net         128.167.254.195                !
!   archie.rutgers.edu      128.6.18.15                    !
!                                                          !
!   archie.au               139.130.4.6                    !
!   archie.funet.fi         128.214.6.102                   !
!   archie.ncu.edu.tw       140.115.19.24                  !
!   archie.doc.ic.ac.uk     146.169.11.3                   !
!   archie.sogang.ac.kr     163.239.1.11                   !
!                                                          !
! o Questions/comments to archie-admin@ans.net, site add/delete !
! requests to archie-updates@bunyip.com                    !
!                                                          !
! Client software is available on ftp.ans.net:/pub/archie/clients; !
! documentation in /pub/archie/doc.                        !
*─────────────────────────────────────────────────────────*
# term set to vt100 24 80
archie>
ALT-F10  HELP | ANSI-BBS | FDX | 4800 N81 | LOG CLOSED | PRT OFF | CR | CR
```

Figure 5.14:
The archie
server at
archie.ans.net.

Sometimes when you try to run an Internet service like archie from telnet you will be turned away and told to try again later or to try another server. If too many people are already logged in when you try to connect to archie at archie.and.net you will get an error message screen explaining this to you and listing alternative servers.

To search for programs from the archie server, type **prog** followed by the name of the program. To continue the previous example, type the following:

prog pgp

Then press Enter, and the `archie` server produces its results, the end of which is shown in figure 5.15.

```
     Location: /informatik.public_new/comp/usenet/alt.sources
        DIRECTORY rwxrwxr-x      1024  Apr 28 17:35   pgp
     Location: /informatik.public/comp/usenet/alt.sources
        DIRECTORY rwxrwxr-x       512  Dec  9  1992   pgp

Host ftp.uni-kl.de   (131.246.9.95)
Last updated 05:00  8 Jun 1993

     Location: /pub1/unix/security
        DIRECTORY rwxrwxr-x       512  Feb 24 19:24   pgp

Host walton.maths.tcd.ie   (134.226.81.10)
Last updated 09:45  7 May 1993

     Location: /src/misc/pgp-2.0/src
        FILE        rwxr-xr-x   316640  Oct 18  1992   pgp

Host ftp.luth.se   (130.240.18.2)
Last updated 08:07  7 May 1993

     Location: /pub/infosystems
        DIRECTORY rwxr-xr-x       512  Jan 27 12:59   pgp

archie>
ALT-F10   HELP  | ANSI-BBS | FDX |  4800 N81 | LOG CLOSED | PRT OFF | CR   | CR
```

Figure 5.15:

Search for `pgp` at the `archie` server.

Note that the `archie` server also has a help function that can explain how to use other `archie` commands.

To exit the `archie` server, type **quit** and press Enter.

Other `archie` servers include:

> quiche.cs.mcgill.ca (132.206.2.3 or 132.206.51.1)

> archie.rutgers.edu

Two other useful `archie` server commands are set `maxhits` and `whatis`. Typing **set maxhits 100** and pressing Enter at the `archie` server prompt tells `archie` to stop after it finds more than 100 occurrences of the file. This is useful in case you type in a search criterion that is too broad.

If you are running `archie` directly on your Internet system—that is, you did not need to use `telnet` to get to an `archie` server—the equivalent command is `-m100`. That is, to find all the programs with `pgp` in their names, but no more than 100 of them, you type:

> **archie -s -m100 pgp**

The whatis *keyword* command searches a database of program descriptions looking for the *keyword* you type in. However, not all programs are in that database. For example, typing the following:

```
whatis pgp
```

and pressing Enter gives a response indicating that the keyword pgp was not found.

Note that whatis is not always available if you are running archie directly on your Internet system.

Using www

The www, or World-Wide Web, program is, like gopher, an interface to many other information repositories on the Internet. However, it is organized by *hypertext*, or links between items.

As a program, www is organized by a series of keywords and index numbers. You can do searches based on keywords, or jump to a particular index number. You also can do keyword searches from within the area referenced by a particular index number.

Like gopher and archie, some Internet systems offer a www client on them, in which case you can run it by typing **www** and pressing Enter. If this software is not offered by your Internet system, you will need to use telnet to reach the www server. To log on to the www server, type:

```
telnet info.cern.ch
```

Then press Enter.

Another telnet entrance point for www can be accessed by typing:

```
telnet eies2.njit.edu
```

You then press Enter, and log in as **www**.

Whether you run www on your Internet machine or use telnet to reach a www server, you will get a screen like that shown in figure 5.16.

```
                                                          Overview of the Web
                            GENERAL OVERVIEW
        There is no "top" to the World-Wide Web. You can look at it from many points
        of view. If you have no other bias, here are some places to start:

        by Subject[1]            A classification by subject of interest. Incomplete
                                 but easiest to use.

        by Type[2]               Looking by type of service (access protocol, etc) may
                                 allow to find things if you know what you are looking
                                 for.

        About WWW[3]             About the World-Wide Web global information sharing
                                 project

    Starting somewhere else

        To use a different default page, perhaps one representing your field of
        interest, see  "customizing your home page"[4].

    What happened to CERN?
    1-6, <RETURN> for more, Quit, or Help:
     ALT-F10  HELP  | ANSI-BBS |  FDX  |  4800 N81  |  LOG CLOSED  | PRT OFF |  CR   |   CR
```

Figure 5.16:

The opening www
screen.

As you can see, this opening screen lists a number of keywords,
each with a number in brackets after it. You can type the number
shown in these brackets to jump to that information area and see
what further information is available there. For example, there is
a Subject keyword, with [1] after it. If you type **1** at the prompt,
you will get a subject index for www (see fig. 5.17).

```
                    The World-Wide Web Virtual Library: Subject Catalogue (45/69)
        Geography              World maps[14] . CIA World Fact Book[15] , India:
                               Miscellaneous information[16] , Thai-Yunnan: Davis
                               collection[17] ,

        History                See Literature & Art[18] , Newsgroup soc.history[19]

        Law[20]                US Copyright law[21] ., Uniform Commercial Code[22] ,
                               etc, NASDAQ Finance Executive Journal[23] .

        Libraries[24]          Lists of online catalogues etc.

        Literature & Art[25]   separate list.

        Mathematics            CIRM library[26] (french). The  International
                               Journal  of Analytical and Experimental Modal
                               Analysis[27]

        Meteorology            US weather[28] , state by state.  Satelite Images
                               [29]. weather index[30] .

        Music                  MIDI interfacing[31] ,  Song lyrics[32] (apparently
                               disabled for copyright reasons)
    1-47, Back, Up, <RETURN> for more, Quit, or Help:
     ALT-F10  HELP  | ANSI-BBS |  FDX  |  4800 N81  |  LOG CLOSED  | PRT OFF |  CR   |   CR
```

Figure 5.17:

The www index
screen. (This
information is
several pages
long; only a portion
of it is shown.)

Now you can see a number of other entries, all with keywords and numbers. One of the entries is Literature & Art, with the number 25 after it in brackets; typing **25** and then pressing Enter gets you to the screen shown in figure 5.18.

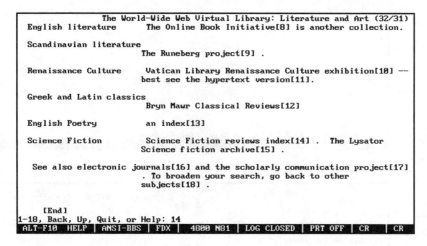

```
                The World-Wide Web Virtual Library: Literature and Art (32/31)
English literature       The Online Book Initiative[8] is another collection.

Scandinavian literature
                         The Runeberg project[9] .

Renaissance Culture      Vatican Library Renaissance Culture exhibition[10] --
                         best see the hypertext version[11].

Greek and Latin classics
                         Bryn Mawr Classical Reviews[12]

English Poetry           an index[13]

Science Fiction          Science Fiction reviews index[14] .  The Lysator
                         Science fiction archive[15] .

  See also electronic journals[16] and the scholarly communication project[17]
                  . To broaden your search, go back to other
                  subjects[18] .


      [End]
1-18, Back, Up, Quit, or Help: 14
ALT-F10  HELP | ANSI-BBS | FDX  |  4800 N81 | LOG CLOSED | PRT OFF | CR   |   CR
```

Figure 5.18:

The Literature & Arts screen.

Here you have several choices, one of which is an index of science fiction reviews. Select the Science Fiction reviews index by typing **14**, which is the number in brackets by this choice. Then press return and you will see not another lisitng, but a search screen.

This screen does not show you information, but instead asks you to type in a keyword for which to search. To find a listing of all the works by Harlan Ellison, for example, you type **find Ellison** at the prompt and press Enter (see fig. 5.19, bottom line).

You get the same results if you search for "ellison" or "Ellison." The find command in www is not case-sensitive. Finally, www gives you the list of all the resources it has available that include the word Ellison. (Actually, some of these could include works by literary Ellisons other than Harlan; for example, perhaps some of these references are to Ralph Ellison's book *The Invisible Man.*) This screen is shown in figure 5.20.

```
                                                      sf-reviews index
                              SF-REVIEWS

      Specify search words.
        [End]
```

```
FIND <keywords>, Back, Quit, or Help: find Ellison
ALT-F10  HELP  | ANSI-BBS  |  FDX  |  4800 N81  | LOG CLOSED | PRT OFF |  CR   |  CR
```

Figure 5.19:

The Science Fiction-Reviews index screen.

```
                                                  Ellison (in sf-reviews)
                              ELLISON

     Index sf-reviews contains the following 19 items relevant to 'Ellison'. The
     first figure for each entry is its relative score, the second the number of
     lines in the item.

1000    121  warda@vax. Re: Review: ALIEN SEX, edited by Ellen Datlow[1]
1000    152  ecl@mtgzy. Re: PRAYERS TO BROKEN STONES by Dan Simmons[2]
 858    523  moh2@midwa Re: Alternate Sexuality in SF/F[3]
 715    381  djdaneh@pb Re: WELCOME TO REC.ARTS.SF.REVIEWS[4]
 715    382  djdaneh@pb Re: WELCOME TO REC.ARTS.SF.REVIEWS[5]
 715    394  djdaneh@pb Re: Welcome to rec.arts.sf.reviews[6]
 715     57  wex@media. Re: Review of BIMBOS OF THE DEATH SUN[7]
 715    146  pteich@cay Re: Review:  Poul Anderson's THE BOAT OF A MILLION
YEARS[8]
 715    254  djdaneh@pa Re: Welcome to rec.arts.sf-reviews[9]
 715     84  throopw@sh Re: REVIEW:  Soothsayer by Mike Resnick[10]
 715    322  djdaneh@pb Re: Welcome to rec.arts.sf.reviews (Last update
11/91)[11]
 715     89  djdaneh@pb Re: KINSHIP WITH THE STARS by Poul Anderson[12]
 715     95  ecl@mtgzy. Re: Corrected repost -- KINSHIP WITH THE STARS by Poul
FIND <keywords>, 1-19, Back, <RETURN> for more, Quit, or Help:
ALT-F10  HELP  | ANSI-BBS  |  FDX  |  4800 N81  | LOG CLOSED | PRT OFF |  CR   |  CR
```

Figure 5.20:

The list of science fiction reviews with the word Ellison in them.

Here, you can choose any of these reviews by typing in the number in brackets at the end of each listing and then pressing Enter.

BREAKING THE SPEED LIMIT

Services such as www are changing so fast that the best way for you to find out what is available on them is to log on and check.

Note, too, that a number of white pages directories are available through www.

To back up through the list of menus, type **b** and press Enter. Note that each menu has its own list of index numbers associated with it—for example, if you want to get back to the main index, you cannot simply type **1** at the Science Fiction screen to do so; you must back up through the screens to reach the index. However, you can type **home** and press Enter to reach the initial www screen, the one you saw when you first ran www.

To exit www, type **quit** and press Enter.

Using WAIS

WAIS, or the Wide Area Information Server system, is less intuitive to use than some of the other search methods, so you might want to try those first. WAIS is best at searches for various kinds of academic information.

Like the other search methods discussed so far, WAIS offers a command to use on your Internet system and, if that command is not available, the ability to connect to a WAIS server using telnet.

Using the waissearch Command

The command to use on your Internet system for WAIS is waissearch. The format of the command is as follows:

```
waissearch -h waissource -p portnumber keyword
```

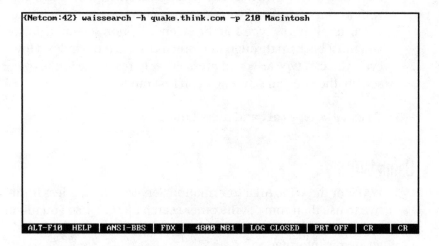
waissource is the WAIS host server to be searched (generally, `quake.think.com`), *portnumber* is the special entry point for WAIS searches (remember that port numbers were discussed in Chapter 3), and *keyword* is the word for which you want to search the WAIS databases.

If you want to search the `quake.think.com` WAIS server for all the entries on the Macintosh, for example, you would type the command as shown in figure 5.21.

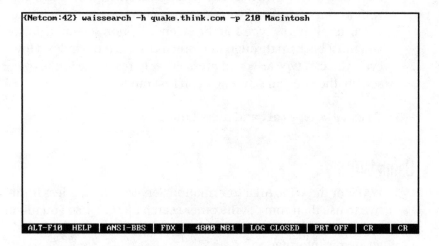

```
{Netcom:42} waissearch -h quake.think.com -p 210 Macintosh




















ALT-F10  HELP | ANSI-BBS | FDX |  4800 N81 | LOG CLOSED | PRT OFF | CR  |  CR
```

Figure 5.21:

Using the `waissearch` command.

In the figure, `210` is the port number on `quake.think.com` that specifies a WAIS search. The results you get from this command are shown in figure 5.22.

The `waissearch` command then asks you to type the number of the resource that you want to see. For example, type **1** and press Enter, and you get information like that shown in figure 5.23.

```
{Netcom:42} waissearch -h quake.think.com -p 210 Macintosh

Search Response:
  NumberOfRecordsReturned: 10
   1: Score: 1000, lines:   13 'macintosh-news.src'
   2: Score:  942, lines:   11 'macintosh-tidbits.src'
   3: Score:  412, lines:   61 'academic_email_conf.src'
   4: Score:  353, lines:   78 'ANU-Asian-Computing.src'
   5: Score:  353, lines:   12 'comp.sys.mac.programmer.src'
   6: Score:  353, lines:  131 'internet-mail.src'
   7: Score:  353, lines:   15 'mac.FAQ.src'
   8: Score:  353, lines:   15 'merit-archive-mac.src'
   9: Score:  353, lines:   76 'nrao-fits.src'
  10: Score:  353, lines:   27 'tcl-talk.src'

View document number [type 0 or q to quit]:
```

```
ALT-F10  HELP | ANSI-BBS | FDX |  4800 N81 | LOG CLOSED | PRT OFF | CR |  CR
```

Figure 5.22:

Results from the `waissearch` command.

```
   5: Score:  353, lines:   12 'comp.sys.mac.programmer.src'
   6: Score:  353, lines:  131 'internet-mail.src'
   7: Score:  353, lines:   15 'mac.FAQ.src'
   8: Score:  353, lines:   15 'merit-archive-mac.src'
   9: Score:  353, lines:   76 'nrao-fits.src'
  10: Score:  353, lines:   27 'tcl-talk.src'

View document number [type 0 or q to quit]: 1
Headline: macintosh-news.src
(:source
 :version  3
 :ip-address "131.239.2.100"
 :ip-name "cmns-moon.think.com"
 :tcp-port 210
 :database-name "MAC CSMP TIDB"
 :maintainer "bug-public@think.com"
 :description
 "This source combines several publications of interest to Macintosh
  users: The info-mac digest (info-mac@sumex-aim.stanford.edu), Michael
  Kelly's comp.sys.mac.programmer digest, and Adam Engst's TidBITS
  electronic magazine for the Macintosh."
 )

View document number [type 0 or q to quit]:
```

```
ALT-F10  HELP | ANSI-BBS | FDX |  4800 N81 | LOG CLOSED | PRT OFF | CR |  CR
```

Figure 5.23:

Selecting a result from `waissearch`.

As you can see, `waissearch` tells you where you can find this repository of Macintosh information and how to get to it.

To exit the selection command, type **q**. Then, to exit the search command, type **q** again.

AVOID THE WAIS TRAFFIC JAM

Be sure you type **q** twice. If you type **q** and then press Enter, WAIS will give you a list of all the databases in its files—several hundred of them. You can stop this assault by typing **^C** (that is, pressing Ctrl and C simultaneously), but it may take a while for the command to make its way through to the WAIS server.

Using `telnet` To Reach WAIS

The WAIS server is located at `quake.think.com`. You can log onto it with `telnet` and then log in as `wais`, as shown in figure 5.24.

```
{Netcom:44} telnet quake.think.com
Trying...
Connected to quake.think.com.
Escape character is '^]'.


SunOS UNIX (quake)

login: wais
Last login: Mon Jul 19 15:21:10 from netcom3.netcom.c
SunOS Release 4.1.1 (QUAKE) #3: Tue Jul 7 11:09:01 PDT 1992

Welcome to swais.
Please type user identifier (optional, i.e user@host): slf@netcom.netcom.com
TERM = (vt100)




ALT-F10  HELP  | ANSI-BBS | FDX | 4800 N81 | LOG CLOSED | PRT OFF |  CR  |  CR
```

Figure 5.24:

Using `telnet` to reach the WAIS server.

As with an anonymous `ftp` server, the WAIS server asks you to type your Internet address to help track use. The WAIS server then asks you to tell it what kind of terminal you have, with VT100 being the default. After you do that, WAIS starts displaying all the information sources it has, one screen at a time. But how do you find the right information source to search? There are hundreds.

To search for a particular information source, type **/**, and WAIS will ask you for a keyword to use on a source search. To search for information sources about Usenet on the Macintosh, for

example, first find what information sources handle the
Macintosh. Type / **Macintosh** and press Enter when WAIS asks you
what source you're looking for (see fig. 5.25).

```
SWAIS                           Source Selection           Sources: 463
  #             Server                      Source             Cost
001: [         archie.au]  aarnet-resource-guide             Free
002: [      munin.ub2.lu.se]  academic_email_conf            Free
003: [wraith.cs.uow.edu.au]  acronyms                        Free
004: [     archive.orst.edu]  aeronautics                    Free
005: [ ftp.cs.colorado.edu]  aftp-cs-colorado-edu            Free
006: [nostromo.oes.orst.ed]  agricultural-market-news        Free
007: [     archive.orst.edu]  alt.drugs                      Free
008: [      wais.oit.unc.edu]  alt.gopher                    Free
009: [sun-wais.oit.unc.edu]  alt.sys.sun                     Free
010: [      wais.oit.unc.edu]  alt.wais                      Free
011: [alfred.ccs.carleton.]  amiga-slip                      Free
012: [      munin.ub2.lu.se]  amiga_fish_contents            Free
013: [      coombs.anu.edu.au]  ANU-Aboriginal-Studies       $0.00/minute
014: [      coombs.anu.edu.au]  ANU-Asian-Computing          $0.00/minute
015: [      coombs.anu.edu.au]  ANU-Asian-Religions          $0.00/minute
016: [       150.203.76.2]  ANU-CAUT-Academics               $0.00/minute
017: [      coombs.anu.edu.au]  ANU-CAUT-Projects            $0.00/minute
018: [      coombs.anu.edu.au]  ANU-Coombspapers-Index       $0.00/minute

Source Name: Macintosh

<space> selects, w for keywords, arrows move, <return> searches, q quits, or ?
 ALT-F10  HELP | ANSI-BBS | FDX |  4800 N81 | LOG CLOSED | PRT OFF | CR  |  CR
```

Figure 5.25:

Searching for
Macintosh
information
sources.

To go on to the next step in the search, select information sources
by using your cursor key to move to the information sources and
then select them by pressing the spacebar. WAIS will indicate that
these information sources have been chosen by displaying an
asterisk (*). Choose two of these sources.

Now that you have chosen two sources of Macintosh information,
you can search for references to Usenet within those sources by
pressing Enter to indicate that you want to begin a search. WAIS
then asks you what keywords you wish to search for; type **Usenet**
and press Enter to begin the search, as shown in figure 5.26.

When you do that, WAIS will tell you how many references it
found with the word Usenet, as shown in figure 5.27 (see the last
line on-screen).

```
SWAIS                           Source Selection           Sources: 463
  #              Server                    Source                 Cost
271:  [         wais.cic.net]  kidsnet                            Free
272:  [       sunsite.unc.edu]  linux-addresses                   Free
273:  [       sunSITE.unc.edu]  linux-faq                         Free
274:  [       sunSITE.unc.edu]  linux-gcc-faq                     Free
275:  [       sunSITE.unc.edu]  linux-mail-faq                    Free
276:  [       sunSITE.unc.edu]  linux-net-faq                     Free
277:  [       sunSITE.unc.edu]  linux-software-map                Free
278:  [         wais.cic.net]  lists                              Free
279:  [hermes.ecn.purdue.ed]  livestock                          Free
280:  [      munin.ub2.lu.se]  lolita-dator                       Free
281:  [      munin.ub2.lu.se]  lolita-miljo                       Free
282:  [         gopher.uwo.ca]  london-free-press-regional-inde   Free
283:  [       zenon.inria.fr]  lp-bibtex-zenon-inria-fr           Free
284:  [      wais.fct.unl.pt]  lp-proceedings                     Free
285:  [          cs.uwp.edu]  lyrics                              Free
286:  [     next2.oit.unc.edu]  mac.FAQ                           Free
287: * [ cmns-moon.think.com]  macintosh-news                     Free
288: * [ cmns-moon.think.com]  macintosh-tidbits                  Free

Keywords: Usenet

Enter keywords with spaces between them; <return> to search; ^C to cancel
ALT-F10  HELP | ANSI-BBS | FDX |  4800 N81 | LOG CLOSED | PRT OFF | CR |  CR
```

Figure 5.26:

Starting a WAIS search in an information source.

```
SWAIS                           Source Selection           Sources: 463
  #              Server                    Source                 Cost
271:  [         wais.cic.net]  kidsnet                            Free
272:  [      s   site.unc.edu]  linux-addresses                   Free
273:  [       sunSITE.unc.edu]  linux-faq                         Free
274:  [       sunSITE.unc.edu]  linux-gcc-faq                     Free
275:  [       sunSITE.unc.edu]  linux-mail-faq                    Free
276:  [       sunSITE.unc.edu]  linux-net-faq                     Free
277:  [       sunSITE.unc.edu]  linux-software-map                Free
278:  [         wais.cic.net]  lists                              Free
279:  [hermes.ecn.purdue.ed]  livestock                          Free
280:  [      munin.ub2.lu.se]  lolita-dator                       Free
281:  [      munin.ub2.lu.se]  lolita-miljo                       Free
282:  [         gopher.uwo.ca]  london-free-press-regional-inde   Free
283:  [       zenon.inria.fr]  lp-bibtex-zenon-inria-fr           Free
284:  [      wais.fct.unl.pt]  lp-proceedings                     Free
285:  [          cs.uwp.edu]  lyrics                              Free
286:  [     next2.oit.unc.edu]  mac.FAQ                           Free
287: * [ cmns-moon.think.com]  macintosh-news                     Free
288: * [ cmns-moon.think.com]  macintosh-tidbits                  Free

Keywords: Internet

Found 40 items.
ALT-F10  HELP | ANSI-BBS | FDX |  4800 N81 | LOG CLOSED | PRT OFF | CR |  CR
```

Figure 5.27:

Number of references found.

Then, WAIS will give you a list of references within the two Macintosh sources that contain the word Usenet, as shown in figure 5.28.

You can look at any of these entries by typing in the number and pressing the spacebar. For example, WAIS is already highlighting the first entry; you can display it by pressing the spacebar. WAIS will then show you this reference (see fig. 5.29).

```
SWAIS                              Search Results                    Items: 40
   #     Score     Source                    Title                        Lines
001:    [1000] (cmns-moon.think) TidBITS#07: CompuServe Censoring  ------     43
002:    [1000] (cmns-moon.think) Info-Mac Digest V9 #305:  SPARC .au file     22
003:    [1000] (cmns-moon.think) Info-Mac Digest V9 257:   USENET and the     35
004:    [1000] (cmns-moon.think) Info-Mac Digest V8 #201:  COMP.SOURCES.M     25
005:    [ 978] (cmns-moon.think) TidBITS#07: CompuServe Censoring  ------     43
006:    [ 955] (cmns-moon.think) Info-Mac Digest V11 #48:  [*] no subject    149
007:    [ 954] (cmns-moon.think) TidBITS#05: CheckFree Security Checks  -     41
008:    [ 954] (cmns-moon.think) TidBITS#02: White Knight Blackened  ----     34
009:    [ 932] (cmns-moon.think) Info-Mac Digest V11 #144:  email address     31
010:    [ 932] (cmns-moon.think) Info-Mac Digest V11 #135:  Can't backgro     35
011:    [ 932] (cmns-moon.think) TidBITS#05: CheckFree Security Checks  -     41
012:    [ 932] (cmns-moon.think) TidBITS#02: White Knight Blackened  ----     34
013:    [ 932] (cmns-moon.think) Comp.Sys.Mac.Programmer:      UPMG II  From    43
014:    [ 932] (cmns-moon.think) Info-Mac Digest V10 #38:  [*] TidBITS#10     35
015:    [ 907] (cmns-moon.think) TidBITS#04: Topic Real-Time  -----------     45
016:    [ 887] (cmns-moon.think) Info-Mac Digest V11 #144:  Better ways o     43
017:    [ 887] (cmns-moon.think) Info-Mac Digest V11 #140:  [*] UULite 1.     40
018:    [ 887] (cmns-moon.think) Info-Mac Digest V11 #129:  SpeedyCD & FW     36


<space> selects, arrows move, w for keywords, s for sources, ? for help
 ALT-F10  HELP | ANSI-BBS | FDX | 4800 N81 | LOG CLOSED | PRT OFF | CR |  CR
```

Figure 5.28:

The results of a
WAIS search.

```
0000063TIDB
900504
TidBITS electronic magazine for the Macintosh
Copyright 1990-1992 Adam & Tonya Engst. Non-profit, non-commercial
publications may reprint articles if full credit is given.


TidBITS#07: CompuServe Censoring

-------------------
   Several people on Usenet report that CompuServe has killed its
   National Bulletin Board service as of June 1st, 1990. In its place
   is a new bulletin board service that charges $1.00 per line. The
   cost doesn't seem to be the problem, though. Instead CompuServe
   has instituted a censorship policy on all ads, judging them for
   appropriateness, however broad that might be. An exact definition
   was not forthcoming from CompuServe, but materials of a sexual
   nature are definitely prohibited. Luckily, this policy seems only
   to affect the open areas such as the data libraries and
   advertisements; closed areas are still uncensored.

   Despite the irritation that some people will no doubt feel at this
    new policy, CompuServe is not to blame. They are merely protecting
    themselves from prosecution. One Usenet member suggests that
:
 ALT-F10  HELP | ANSI-BBS | FDX | 4800 N81 | LOG CLOSED | PRT OFF | CR |  CR
```

Figure 5.29:

Selecting a
reference.

When WAIS reaches the end of the reference, it displays the word
(END). At this point, you type **q** to exit the reference, and WAIS will
tell you to press any key to get back to the list of references. The
end of the reference is shown in figure 5.30.

```
Despite the irritation that some people will no doubt feel at this
 new policy, CompuServe is not to blame. They are merely protecting
themselves from prosecution. One Usenet member suggests that
CompuServe might be subject to local and state laws in areas
wherever a CompuServe dial-up number is located. The greater issue
is why CompuServe feels it necessary to protect themselves that
extent. Interestingly enough, Usenet carries materials that are
almost certain to offend those of the stricter morality, but we
suspect that it would be almost impossible to force Usenet as a
whole to do anything legally, considering the huge and amorphous
structure of the net. CompuServe, as a corporate entity, cannot
ignore the legal manipulations and dangers of the business world.
Pity, since free flow of information requires freedom from
persecution, be it legal or not.

  CompuServe -- 800/848-8990 -- 614/457-8650

Information from:
  Art Gentry -- gentry@kcdev.UUCP
  Leonard Erickson -- leonard@qiclab.UUCP


(END)
ALT-F10  HELP  | ANSI-BBS | FDX  |  4800 N81 | LOG CLOSED | PRT OFF | CR  |  CR
```

Figure 5.30:

Exiting a reference.

You can either select another reference, type **s** and press Enter to get back to the list of sources, or type **q** to exit WAIS.

Examining Other Useful Resources from the Net

The Internet is changing so quickly that it is important for you to keep up-to-date on resources and commands you are using. Organizations are adding support for whois all the time, for example; keeping track of new whois supporters makes it easier for you to find users.

One of the best sources on changes to Internet resources is the comp.answers Netnews group. Articles are posted to this Netnews group periodically that give the most current information on, for example, finding source code on the Internet, tracking down a person's e-mail address, or gopher and archie sites.

Another useful list that gets posted to comp.answers is the list of Internet resources. While this list primarily contains information that you can get by using ftp or telnet to reach a particular site, it provides other information as well. There also is a FAQ file about Internet services that is posted periodically.

A concise list of Internet tools and their basic functions is available by logging in with `ftp` anonymously to `ftp.rpi.edu` and downloading the file `pub/communications/internet-tools`. It describes the demonstrations and documentation materials that are available for each tool as well.

The Computer Mediated Communication list, a huge list of information about the Internet—basically, an index to Internet information and services—is available by logging in with `ftp` anonymously to `ftp.rpi.edu` and downloading the file `pub/communications/internet-cmc`. It also lists a number of research organizations associated with the Internet and where to get more information about them, Netnews groups of interest for particular areas, and a bibliography.

Summary

At this point, if you have read this book more or less from cover to cover, you should be familiar with the basic tools for using the Internet. You should have a decent grounding in how to think of the Internet—as a huge complex of interconnected information sources.

You should be familiar with the feel of the Internet—a surprisingly *personal* sensation, yet not so surprising when you consider that the Internet is indeed made up of *people* more than hardware and software. And presumably you have learned how to act courteously to others as you share this interspace.

Above all, if this book has done its job, you've hopefully developed a profound curiosity for exploring what the Internet can do for you, where it can take you. You've been given "pointers" to a number of places where you can find out more. In other words, you have learned to drive and you have a fistful of maps in your glove compartment.

Where do you want to go? It's now that you have to go out there and experience the Internet for all its worth. You might want to start by using the various search tools to find more information about the specific areas of the Internet that interest you. You should also read the appendixes, gleaning information from them. The choice is yours. See you on the Internet.

PDIAL List of Internet Providers

Providers with Wide Area Access

The following is a list of wide area access providers on the Internet:

> PDN delphi, holonet, michnet, portal, psi-gds, psilink, well, world, 800 class, cns, crl, csn, dial-n-cerf-usa, jvnc, OARnet

"PDN" means the provider is accessible through a public data network (check the listings following for which network); note that many PDNs listed offer access outside North America as well as within North America. Check with the provider or the PDN for more details.

"800" means the provider is accessible via a "toll-free" U.S. phone number. The phone company will not charge for the call, but the service provider will add a surcharge to cover the cost of the 800 service. This may be more expensive than other long-distance options.

Area Codes for US/Canada Dialins

If you are not local to any of the following providers, it's still likely you are able to access those providers available through a public data network (PDN). Check the preceding section for providers with wide area access.

201 jvnc-tiger

202 express, grebyn

203 jvnc-tiger

206 eskimo, halcyon, netcom, nwnexus

212 mindvox, panix

213 dial-n-cerf, netcom

214 metronet

215 jvnc-tiger, PREPnet

216 OARnet, wariat

301 express, grebyn

303 cns, csn

310 dial-n-cerf, netcom

312 ddsw1

313 michnet, MSen

401 anomaly, ids, jvnc-tiger

408 a2i, netcom, portal

410 express

412 PREPnet, telerama

415 crl, dial-n-cerf, netcom, portal, well

419 OARnet

503 netcom

508 anomaly, nearnet

510 dial-n-cerf, holonet, netcom

513 OARnet

514 CAM.ORG

516 jvnc-tiger

517 michnet

603 nearnet

609 jvnc-tiger

614 OARnet

616 michnet

617 delphi, nearnet, world

619 cyber, dial-n-cerf, netcom

703 express, grebyn

704 rock-concert

707 crl

708 ddsw1

713 sugar

714 dial-n-cerf

717 PREPnet

718 mindvox, panix

719 cns, csn, oldcolo

814 PREPnet

815 ddsw1

818 dial-n-cerf, netcom

906 michnet

908 jvnc-tiger

916 netcom

919 rock-concert

These are area codes local to the dialups, although some prefixes in the area codes listed may not be local to the dialups. Check your phone book or with your phone company.

Most providers listed here are also accessible by packet-switched data services such as PC Pursuit ($30/month for 30 hours off-peak 2400 bps access — call 800-736-1130 for more information), traditional long distance services, and of course, telnet.

Phone Prefixes for International Dialins

If you are not local to any of the following providers, there is still a chance you are able to access those providers available through a public data network (PDN). Check the preceding section for providers with wide area access, and send e-mail to them to ask about availability.

+61 2 connect.com.au

+61 3 connect.com.au

+44 (0)81 ibmpcug

What the PDIAL Is

The following is a list of Internet service providers offering public access dialins and outgoing Internet access (ftp, telnet, etc.). Most of them provide e-mail and Usenet news and other services as well.

If one of these systems is not accessible to you and you need e-mail or Usenet access, but *don't* need ftp or telnet, you have many more public access systems from which to choose. Public access systems without ftp or telnet are *not* in this list, however. See the nixpub (alt.bbs, comp.misc) list and other BBS lists.

Some of these providers offer time-shared access to a shell or BBS program on a computer connected directly to the Internet, through which you can use ftp or telnet to gain access to other systems on the Internet. Usually other services are provided as well. Generally, you need only a modem and terminal or terminal emulator to access these systems. Check for "shell," "bbs," or "menu" on the "services" line.

Other providers connect you directly to the Internet via SLIP or PPP when you dial in. For these you need a computer system capable of running the software to interface with the Internet, e.g., a Unix machine, PC, or Mac. Check for "SLIP," or "PPP" on the services line.

List of Providers

The following is a list of providers with costs, local access areas, and services.

Fees are for personal dialup accounts with outgoing Internet access; most sites have other classes of service with other rate structures as well. Most support e-mail and Netnews along with the listed services.

"Long distance: provided by user" means you need to use services such as PC Pursuit, direct dial long distance, or other long distance services.

a2i

Name	a2i communications
Dialup	408-293-9010 (v.32, v.32 bis) or 408-293-9020 (PEP) 'guest'
Area Codes	408
Local Access	CA: Campbell, Los Altos, Los Gatos, Mountain View, San Jose, Santa Clara, Saratoga, Sunnyvale
Long Distance	provided by user
Services	shell, ftp, telnet, feeds

Fees	$20/month or $45/3 months or $72/6 months
E-mail	info@rahul.net
Voice	n/a
ftp More Info	ftp.rahul.net:/pub/BLURB

anomaly

Name	Anomaly - Rhode Island's Gateway To The Internet
Dialup	401-331-3706 (v.32) or 401-455-0347 (PEP)
Area Codes	401, 508
Local Access	RI: Providence/Seekonk Zone
Long Distance	provided by user
Services	shell, ftp, telnet, SLIP
Fees	Commercial: $125/6 months or $200/year; Educational: $75/6 months or $125/year
E-mail	info@anomaly.sbs.risc.net
Voice	401-273-4669
ftp More Info	anomaly.sbs.risc.net:/anomaly.info/access.zip

CAM.ORG

Name	Communications Accessibles Montreal
Dialup	514-281-5601 (v.32 bis, HST) 514-738-3664 (PEP), 514-923-2103 (ZyXeL 19.2K) 514-466-0592 (v.32)
Area codes	514
Local Access	QC: Montreal, Laval, South-Shore, West-Island
Long Distance	provided by user
Services	shell, ftp, telnet, feeds, SLIP, PPP, FAX gateway
Fees	$25/month Cdn.

E-mail	info@CAM.ORG
Voice	514-923-2102
ftp More Info	n/a

class

Name	Cooperative Library Agency for Systems and Services
Dialup	contact for number; NOTE: CLASS serves libraries/information distributors only
Area Codes	800
Local Access	anywhere (800) service is available
Long Distance	included
Services	ftp, telnet, gopher, wais, hytelnet
Fees	$10.50/hour + $150/year for first account + $50/year each additional account + $135/year CLASS membership
E-mail	class@class.org
Voice	800-488-4559
Fax	408-453-5379
ftp More Info	n/a

cns

Name	Community News Service
Dialup	719-520-1700 id 'new', passwd 'newuser'
Area Codes	303, 719, 800
Local Access	CO: Colorado Springs, Denver; continental US/800
Long Distance	800 or provided by user
Services	Unix shell, e-mail, ftp, telnet, irc, USENET, Clarinet, gopher

Fees	$1/hour; $10/month minimum + $35 signup
E-mail	klaus@cscns.com
Voice	719-579-9120
ftp More Info	n/a

connect.com.au

Name	connect.com.au pty ltd
Dialup	contact for number
Area Codes	+61 3, +61 2
Local Access	Australia: Melbourne, Sydney
Long Distance	provided by user
Services	SLIP, PPP, ISDN, uucp, ftp, telnet, NTP, FTPmail
Fees	AUS$2000/year (1 hour/day), 10% discount for AUUG members; other billing negotiable
E-mail	connect@connect.com.au
Voice	+61 3 5282239
Fax	+61 3 5285887
ftp More Info	ftp.connect.com.au

crl

Name	CR Laboratories Dialup Internet Access
Dialup	415-389-UNIX
Area codes	415, 707, 800
Local Access	CA: San Francisco Bay Area; continental US/800
Long Distance	800 or provided by user
Services	shell, ftp, telnet, feeds, SLIP, WAIS
Fees	$19.50/month + $15.00 signup

E-mail	info@crl.com
Voice	415-381-2800
ftp More Info	n/a

csn

Name	Colorado SuperNet, Inc.
Dialup	contact for number
Area Codes	303, 719, 800
Local Access	CO: Alamosa, Boulder/Denver, Colorado Springs, Durango, Fort Collins, Frisco, Glenwood Springs/Aspen, Grand Junction, Greeley, Gunnison, Pueblo, Telluride; anywhere 800 service is available
Long Distance	provided by user or 800
Services	shell or menu, uucp, SLIP, 56K, ISDN, T1; ftp, telnet, irc, gopher, WAIS, domains, anonymous ftp space, e-mail-to-fax
Fees	$1/hour off-peak, $3/hour peak ($250 max/month) + $20 signup, $5/hr surcharge for 800 use
E-mail	info@csn.org
Voice	303-273-3471
Fax	303-273-3475
ftp More Info	csn.org:/CSN/reports/DialinInfo.txt off-peak midnight to 6am

cyber

Name	The Cyberspace Station
Dialup	(619) 634-1376 'guest'
Area Codes	619
Local Access	CA: San Diego

Long Distance	provided by user
Services	shell, ftp, telnet, irc
Fees	$15/month + $10 startup or $60 for six months
E-mail	help@cyber.net
Voice	n/a
ftp More Info	n/a

ddsw1

Name	'ddsw1', MCSNet
Dialup	(312) 248-0900 V.32bis/V.32, 248-6295 (PEP), follow prompts
Area Codes	312, 708, 815
Local Access	IL: Chicago
Long Distance	provided by user
Services	shell, ftp, telnet, feeds, e-mail, irc, gopher
Fees	$25/month or $65/3 months
E-mail	info@ddsw1.mcs.com
Voice	n/a
ftp More Info	n/a

delphi

Name	DELPHI
Dialup	(800) 365-4636 'JOINDELPHI password:INTERNETSIG'
Area Codes	617, PDN
Local Access	MA: Boston; KS: Kansas City
Long Distance	Sprintnet or Tymnet: $9/hour weekday business hours, no charge nights and weekends
Services	ftp, telnet, feeds, user groups, wire services, member conferencing

Fees	$10/month for 4 hours or $20/month for 20 hours + $3/month for Internet services
E-mail	walthowe@delphi.com
Voice	800-544-4005
ftp More Info	n/a

dial-n-cerf

Name	DIAL n' CERF or DIAL n' CERF AYC
Dialup	contact for number
Area Codes	213, 310, 415, 510, 619, 714, 818
Local Access	CA: Los Angeles, Oakland, San Diego, Irvine, Pasadena, Palo Alto
Long Distance	provided by user
Services	shell, menu, irc, ftp, hytelnet, gopher, WAIS, WWW, terminal service, SLIP
Fees	$5/hour ($3/hour on weekend) + $20/month + $50 startup OR $250/month flat for AYC
E-mail	help@cerf.net
Voice	800-876-2373 or 619-455-3900
ftp More Info	nic.cerf.net:/cerfnet/dial-n-cerf/off-peak Weekend: 5 p.m. Friday to 5 p.m. Sunday

dial-n-cerf-usa

Name	DIAL n' CERF USA
Dialup	contact for number
Area Codes	800
Local Access	anywhere (800) service is available
Long Distance	included
Services	shell, menu, irc, ftp, hytelnet, gopher, WAIS, WWW, terminal service, SLIP

Fees	$10/hour ($8/hour on weekend) + $20/month
E-mail	help@cerf.net
Voice	800-876-2373 or 619-455-3900
ftp More Info	nic.cerf.net:/cerfnet/dial-n-cerf/off-peak Weekend: 5 p.m. Friday to 5 p.m. Sunday

eskimo

Name	Eskimo North
Dialup	206-367-3837 at 300-2400 bps, 206-362-6731 for 9600/14.4k, 206-742-1150 World Blazer
Area Codes	206
Local Access	WA: Seattle, Everett
Long Distance	provided by user
Services	shell, ftp, telnet
Fees	$10/month or $96/year
E-mail	nanook@eskimo.com
Voice	206-367-7457
ftp More Info	n/a

express

Name	Express Access - Online Communications Service
Dialup	301-220-0462, 410-766-1855 'new'
Area Codes	202, 301, 410, 703
Local Access	Northern VA, Baltimore, MD, Washington, D.C.
Long Distance	provided by user
Services	shell, ftp, telnet, irc
Fees	$25/month or $250/year

E-mail	info@digex.com
Voice	301-220-2020
ftp More Info	n/a

grebyn

Name	Grebyn Corporation
Dialup	703-281-7997, 'apply'
Area Codes	202, 301, 703
Local Access	Northern VA, Southern MD, Washington, D.C.
Long Distance	provided by user
Services	shell, ftp, telnet
Fees	$30/month
E-mail	info@grebyn.com
Voice	703-281-2194
ftp More Info	n/a

halcyon

Name	Halcyon
Dialup	(206) 382-6245 'new', 8N1
Area Codes	206
Local Access	Seattle, WA
Long Distance	provided by user
Services	shell, telnet, ftp, bbs, irc, gopher, hytelnet
Fees	$200/year, or $60/quarter + $10 start-up
E-mail	info@halcyon.com
Voice	206-955-1050
ftp More Info	halcyon.com:~/pub/waffle/info

holonet

Name	HoloNet
Dialup	(510) 704-1058
Area Codes	510, PDN
Local Access	Berkeley, CA
Long Distance	[per hour, off-peak/peak] Bay Area: $0.50/ $0.95; PSINet A: $0.95/$1.95; PSINet B: $2.50/ $6.00; Tymnet: $3.75/$7.50
Services	ftp, telnet, irc, games
Fees	$2/hour off-peak, $4/hour peak; $6/month or $60/year minimum
E-mail	info@holonet.net
Voice	510-704-0160
ftp More Info	holonet.net:/info/off-peak 5 p.m. to 8 a.m. + weekends and holidays

ibmpcug

Name	UK PC User Group
Dialup	+44 (0)81 863 6646
Area Codes	+44 (0)81
Local Access	London, England
Long Distance	provided by user
Services	ftp, telnet, bbs, irc, feeds
Fees	GB pounds $15.50/month or $160/year + 10 startup (no time charges)
E-mail	info@ibmpcug.co.uk
Voice	+44 (0)81 863 6646
ftp More Info	n/a

ids

Name	The IDS World Network
Dialup	(401) 884-9002, (401) 785-1067
Area Codes	401
Local Access	East Greenwich, RI; northern RI
Long Distance	provided by user
Services	ftp, telnet, SLIP, feeds, bbs
Fees	$10/month or $50/half year or $100/year
E-mail	sysadmin@ids.net
Voice	401-884-7856
ftp More Info	ids.net:/ids.net

jvnc-tiger

Name	The John von Neumann Computer Network - Dialin' Tiger
Dialup	contact for number
Area Codes	201, 203, 215, 401, 516, 609, 908
Local Access	Princeton & Newark, NJ; Philadelphia, PA; Garden City, NY; Bridgeport, New Haven, & Storrs, CT; Providence, RI
Long Distance	provided by user
Services	ftp, telnet, SLIP, feeds, optional shell
Fees	$99/month + $99 startup (PC or Mac SLIP software included — shell is additional $21/month)
E-mail	info@jvnc.net
Voice	(800) 35-TIGER, (609) 258-2400
ftp More Info	n/a

jvnc

Name	The John von Neumann Computer Network - Tiger Mail & Dialin' Terminal
Dialup	contact for number
Area Codes	800
Local Access	anywhere (800) service is available
Long Distance	included
Services	e-mail and newsfeed or terminal access only
Fees	$19/month + $10/hour + $36 startup (PC or Mac SLIP software included)
E-mail	info@jvnc.net
Voice	(800) 35-TIGER, (609) 258-2400
ftp More Info	n/a

metronet

Name	Texas Metronet
Dialup	214-705-2902 9600bps, 214-705-2917 2400bps, 'info/info' or 'signup/signup'
Area Codes	214
Local Access	TX: Dallas
Long Distance	provided by user
Services	shell, ftp, telnet, feeds, SLIP
Fees	$10-$50/month + $20-$30 startup
E-mail	srl@metronet.com / 73157.1323@compuserve.com / GEnie:S.LINEBARG
Voice	214-401-2800
Fax	214-401-2802 (8 a.m.-5 p.m. CST weekdays)
ftp More Info	n/a

michnet

Name	Merit Network, Inc. — MichNet project
Dialup	contact for number or telnet hermes.merit.edu and type 'help' at 'Which host?' prompt
Area Codes	313, 517, 616, 906, PDN
Local Access	Michigan; Boston, MA; Washinton, D.C.
Long Distance	SprintNet, Autonet, Michigan Bell packet-switch network
Services	telnet, SLIP, PPP, outbound SprintNet, Autonet and Ann Arbor dialout
Fees	$35/month + $40 signup ($10/month for K-12 & libraries in Michigan)
E-mail	info@merit.edu
Voice	313-764-9430
ftp More Info	nic.merit.edu:/

mindvox

Name	MindVOX
Dialup	(212) 988-5030 'mindvox' 'guest'
Area Codes	212, 718
Local Access	NY: New York City
Long Distance	provided by user
Services	conferencing system ftp, telnet, irc, gopher, hytelnet, Archives, BBS
Fees	$15-$20/month, no startup
E-mail	info@phantom.com
Voice	212-988-5987
ftp More Info	n/a

MSen

Name	MSen
Dialup	contact for number
Area Codes	313
Local Access	All of SE Michigan (313)
Long Distance	provided by user
Services	shell, WAIS, gopher, telnet, ftp, SLIP, PPP, IRC, WWW, Picospan BBS, ftp space
Fees	$20/month; $20 startup
E-mail	info@msen.com
Voice	313-998-4562
Fax	313-998-4563
ftp More Info	ftp.msen.com:/pub/vendor/msen

nearnet

Name	NEARnet
Dialup	contact for numbers
Area codes	508, 603, 617
Local Access	Boston, MA; Nashua, NH
Long Distance	provided by user
Services	SLIP, e-mail, feeds, dns
Fees	$250/month
E-mail	nearnet-join@nic.near.net
Voice	617-873-8730
ftp More Info	nic.near.net:/docs

netcom

Name	Netcom Online Communication Services
Dialup	(206) 527-5992, (310) 842-8835, (408) 241-9760, (408) 459-9851, (415) 328-9940, (415) 985-5650, (503) 626-6833, (510) 426-6610, (510) 865-9004, (619) 234-0524, (916) 965-1371
Area Codes	206, 213, 310, 408, 415, 503, 510, 619, 818, 916
Local Access	CA: SF Bay Area (5 POPs), Sacramento, Santa Cruz, Los Angeles, San Diego; OR: Portland; WA: Seattle (May 1)
Long Distance	provided by user
Services	shell, ftp, telnet, irc, WAIS, gopher, SLIP/PPP, ftp space, feeds, dns
Fees	$19.50/month + $15.00 signup
E-mail	info@netcom.com
Voice	408-554-UNIX
ftp More Info	n/a

nwnexus

Name	Northwest Nexus Inc.
Dialup	contact for numbers
Area Codes	206
Local Access	WA: Seattle
Long Distance	provided by user
Services	uucp, SLIP, PPP, feeds, dns
Fees	$10/month for first 10 hours + $3/hr; $20 start-up
E-mail	info@nwnexus.wa.com
Voice	206-455-3505
ftp More Info	nwnexus.wa.com:/NWNEXUS.info.txt

OARnet

Name	OARnet
Dialup	send e-mail to nic@oar.net
Area Codes	216, 419, 513, 614, 800
Local Access	OH: Columbus, Cincinnati, Cleveland, Dayton
Long Distance	800 service
Services	e-mail, ftp, w3telnet, newsfeed
Fees	$4/hr to $330/month; call for code or send e-mail
E-mail	nic@oar.net
Voice	614-292-8100
Fax	614-292-7168
ftp More Info	n/a

oldcolo

Name	Old Colorado City Communications
Dialup	719-632-4111 'newuser'
Area Codes	719
Local Access	CO: Colorado Springs
Long Distance	provided by user
Services	shell, ftp, telnet, AKCS, home of the NAPLPS conference
Fees	$25/month
E-mail	dave@oldcolo.com / thefox@oldcolo.com
Voice	719-632-4848, 719-593-7575 or 719-636-2040
Fax	719-593-7521
ftp More Info	n/a

panix

Name	PANIX Public Access Unix
Dialup	(212) 787-3100 'newuser'
Area Codes	212, 718
Local Access	New York City, NY
Long Distance	provided by user
Services	shell, ftp, telnet, gopher, WAIS, irc, feeds
Fees	$19/month or $208/year + $40 signup
E-mail	alexis@panix.com, jsb@panix.com
Voice	212-877-4854 [Alexis Rosen], 212-691-1526 [Jim Baumbach]
ftp More Info	n/a

portal

Name	The Portal System
Dialup	(408) 973-8091 high-speed, (408) 725-0561 2400bps; 'info'
Area Codes	408, 415, PDN
Local Access	CA: Cupertino, Mountain View, San Jose
Long Distance	SprintNet: $2.50/hour off-peak, $7-$10/hour peak; Tymnet: $2.50/hour off-peak, $13/hour peak
Services	shell, ftp, telnet, IRC, uucp, feeds, bbs
Fees	$19.95/month + $19.95 signup
E-mail	cs@cup.portal.com, info@portal.com
Voice	408-973-9111
ftp More Info	n/a
Off-Peak	6 p.m. to 7 a.m. + weekends and holidays

PREPnet

Name	PREPnet
Dialup	contact for numbers
Area Codes	215, 412, 717, 814
Local Access	PA: Philadelphia, Pittsburgh, Harrisburg
Long Distance	provided by user
Services	SLIP, terminal service, telnet, ftp
Fees	$1,000/year membership. Equipment-$325 onetime fee plus $40/month
E-mail	prepnet@cmu.edu
Voice	412-268-7870
Fax	412-268-7875
ftp More Info	ftp.prepnet.com:/prepnet/general/

psi-gds

Name	PSI's Global Dialup Service (GDS)
Dialup	send e-mail to numbers-info@psi.com
Area Codes	PDN
Local Access	n/a
Long Distance	included
Services	telnet, rlogin
Fees	$39/month + $39 startup
E-mail	all-info@psi.com, gds-info@psi.com
Voice	703-620-6651
Fax	707-620-4586
ftp More Info	ftp.psi.co7:

psilink

Name	PSILink - Personal Internet Access
Dialup	send e-mail to numbers-info@psi.com
Area Codes	PDN
Local Access	n/a
Long Distance	included
Services	e-mail and newsfeed, ftp
Fees	$29/month + $19 startup (PSILink software included)
E-mail	all-info@psi.com, psilink-info@psi.com
Voice	703-620-6651
Fax	703-620-4586
ftp More Info	ftp.psi.com:/

rock-concert

Name	Rock CONCERT Net
Dialup	contact for number
Area Codes	704, 919
Local Access	NC: Asheville, Chapel Hill, Charlotte, Durham, Greensboro, Greenville, Raleigh, Winston-Salem, Research Triangle Park
Long Distance	provided by user
Services	shell, ftp, telnet, irc, gopher, WAIS, feeds, SLIP
Fees	$30/month + $50 signup
E-mail	info@concert.net
Voice	919-248-1999
ftp More Info	ftp.concert.net

sugar

Name	NeoSoft's Sugar Land Unix
Dialup	713-684-5900
Area Codes	713
Local Access	TX: Houston metro area
Long Distance	provided by user
Services	bbs, shell, ftp, telnet, irc, feeds, uucp
Fees	$29.95/month
E-mail	info@NeoSoft.com
Voice	713-438-4964
ftp More Info	n/a

telerama

Name	Telerama BBS
Dialup	(412) 481-5302 'new'
Area Codes	412
Local Access	PA: Pittsburgh
Long Distance	provided by user
Services	shell, ftp, telnet, feeds, menu, bbs
Fees	$6/month for 10 hours, 60 cents/hour thereafter; no startup
E-mail	info@telerama.pgh.pa.us
Voice	412-481-3505
ftp More Info	telerama.pgh.pa.us:/info/general.info

well

Name	The Whole Earth 'Lectronic Link
Dialup	(415) 332-6106 'newuser'
Area Codes	415, PDN

Local Access	Sausalito, CA
Long Distance	Compuserve Packet Network: $4/hour
Services	shell, ftp, telnet, bbs
Fees	$15.00/month + $2.00/hr
E-mail	info@well.sf.ca.us
Voice	415-332-4335
ftp More Info	n/a

wariat

Name	APK- Public Access UNI* Site
Dialup	216-481-9436 (2400), 216-481-9425 (V.32bis, SuperPEP)
Area Codes	216
Local Access	OH: Cleveland
Long Distance	provided by user
Services	shell, ftp, telnet, irc, gopher, feeds, BBS(Uniboard 1.10)
Fees	$35/monthly, $200/6 months, $20 signup
E-mail	zbig@wariat.org
Voice	216-481-9428
ftp More Info	n/a

world

Name	The World
Dialup	(617) 739-9753 'new'
Area Codes	617, PDN
Local Access	Boston, MA
Long Distance	Compuserve Packet Network: $5.60/hour
Services	shell, ftp, telnet, irc

Fees	$5/month + $2/hr or $20/month for 20 hours
E-mail	office@world.std.com
Voice	617-739-0202
ftp More Info	world.std.com:/world-info/basic.info

The NSFNET Backbone Services Acceptable Use Policy

This appendix lists the acceptable use policies set forth for sections on the Internet that are funded by NSF (National Science Foundation). Other sections may also adhere to these same policies. Be sure to review these policies as you work on the Internet and to query your Internet provider if you have questions regarding them.

General Principle of Acceptable Use Policy

(1). NSFNET Backbone services are provided to support open research and education in and among U.S. research and instructional institutions, plus research arms of for-profit firms when engaged in open scholarly communication and research. Use for other purposes is not acceptable.

Specifically Acceptable Uses:

(2). Communication with foreign researchers and educators in connection with research or instruction, as long as any network that the foreign user employs for such communication provides reciprocal access to U.S. researchers and educators.

(3). Communication and exchange for professional development, to maintain currency, or to debate issues in a field or subfield of knowledge.

(4). Use for disciplinary-society, university-association, government-advisory, or standards activities related to the user's research and instructional activities.

(5). Use in applying for or administering grants or contracts for research or instruction, but not for other fundraising or public relations activities.

(6). Any other administrative communications or activities in direct support of research and instruction.

(7). Announcements of new products or services for use in research or instruction, but not advertising of any kind.

(8). Any traffic originating from a network of another member agency of the Federal Networking Council if the traffic meets the acceptable use policy of that agency.

(9). Communication incidental to otherwise acceptable use, except for illegal or specifically unacceptable use.

Unacceptable Uses:

(10). Use for for-profit activities, unless covered by the General Principle or as a specifically acceptable use.

(11). Extensive use for private or personal business.

This statement applies to use of the the NSFNET Backbone only. NSF expects that connecting networks will formulate their own use policies. The NSF Division of Networking and Communications Research and Infrastructure will resolve any questions about this Policy or its interpretation.

Internet Country Codes

This appendix contains a list based on the ISO (International Organization for Standardization) 3166:1988 standard, updated from one prepared by Mark Horton. Note that the original standard has this same information sorted into about six different orders, both in English and French, so this is an abbreviated version and not to be taken as the entire standard. While it has been checked against the standard, it may possibly contain errors, and the standard and registration newsletters should be verified for any critical application. See Chapter 2 for more information on using these codes.

This copy has been updated through at least July 1993.

Country Number	A 2 Code	A 3 Code
AFGHANISTAN 004	AF	AFG
ALBANIA 008	AL	ALB
ALGERIA 012	DZ	DZA
AMERICAN SAMOA 016	AS	ASM
ANDORRA 020	AD	AND
ANGOLA 024	AO	AGO
ANGUILLA 660	AI	AIA
ANTARCTICA 010	AQ	ATA
ANTIGUA AND BARBUDA 028	AG	ATG
ARGENTINA 032	AR	ARG
ARMENIA 051	AM	ARM
ARUBA 533	AW	ABW
AUSTRALIA 036	AU	AUS
AUSTRIA 040	AT	AUT
AZERBAIJAN 031	AZ	AZE
BAHAMAS 044	BS	BHS
BAHRAIN 048	BH	BHR

Country Number	A 2 Code	A 3 Code
BANGLADESH 050	BD	BGD
BARBADOS 052	BB	BRB
BELARUS 112	BY	BLR
BELGIUM 056	BE	BEL
BELIZE 084	BZ	BLZ
BENIN 204	BJ	BEN
BERMUDA 060	BM	BMU
BHUTAN 064	BT	BTN
BOLIVIA 068	BO	BOL
BOSNIA HERZEGOVINA (N/A)	BA	BIH
BOTSWANA 072	BW	BWA
BOUVET ISLAND 074	BV	BVT
BRAZIL 076	BR	BRA
BRITISH INDIAN OCEAN TERRITORY 086	IO	IOT
BRUNEI DARUSSALAM 096	BN	BRN
BULGARIA 100	BG	BGR

continues

Country Number	A·2 Code	A 3 Code
BURKINA FASO 854	BF	BFA
BURUNDI 108	BI	BDI
BYELORUSSIAN SSR 112	BY	BYS
CAMBODIA 116	KH	KHM
CAMEROON 120	CM	CMR
CANADA 124	CA	CAN
CAPE VERDE 132	CV	CPV
CAYMAN ISLANDS 136	KY	CYM
CENTRAL AFRICAN REPUBLIC 140	CF	CAF
CHAD 148	TD	TCD
CHAGOS ISLANDS (N/A)	IO	N/A
CHILE 152	CL	CHL
CHINA 156	CN	CHN
CHRISTMAS ISLAND 162	CX	CXR
COCOS (KEELING) ISLANDS 166	CC	CCK
COLOMBIA 170	CO	COL
COMOROS 174	KM	COM

Country Number	A 2 Code	A 3 Code
CONGO 178	CG	COG
COOK ISLANDS 184	CK	COK
COSTA RICA 188	CR	CRI
CROATIA (Local name: HRVATSKA) (N/A)	HR	HRV
COTE D'IVOIRE 384	CI	CIV
CUBA 192	CU	CUB
CYPRUS 196	CY	CYP
CZECHOSLOVAKIA 200	CS	CSK
DENMARK 208	DK	DNK
DJIBOUTI 262	DJ	DJI
DOMINICA 212	DM	DMA
DOMINICAN REPUBLIC 214	DO	DOM
EAST TIMOR 626	TP	TMP
ECUADOR 218	EC	ECU
EGYPT 818	EG	EGY
EL SALVADOR 222	SV	SLV

continues

Country Number	A 2 Code	A 3 Code
EQUATORIAL GUINEA 226	GQ	GNQ
ESTONIA 233	EE	EST
ETHIOPIA 230	ET	ETH
FALKLAND ISLANDS (MALVINAS) 238	FK	FLK
FAROE ISLANDS 234	FO	FRO
FIJI 242	FJ	FJI
FINLAND 246	FI	FIN
FRANCE 250	FR	FRA
FRENCH GUIANA 254	GF	GUF
FRENCH POLYNESIA 258	PF	PYF
FRENCH SOUTHERN TERRITORIES 260	TF	ATF
GABON 266	GA	GAB
GAMBIA 270	GM	GMB
GEORGIA 268	GE	GEO
GERMANY 276	DE	DEU
GHANA 288	GH	GHA
GIBRALTAR 292	GI	GIB

Country Number	A 2 Code	A 3 Code
GREECE 300	GR	GRC
GREENLAND 304	GL	GRL
GRENADA 308	GD	GRD
GUADELOUPE 312	GP	GLP
GUAM 316	GU	GUM
GUATEMALA 320	GT	GTM
GUINEA 324	GN	GIN
GUINEA-BISSAU 624	GW	GNB
GUYANA 328	GY	GUY
HAITI 332	HT	HTI
HEARD AND MC DONALD ISLANDS 334	HM	HMD
HONDURAS 340	HN	HND
HONG KONG 344	HK	HKG
HUNGARY 348	HU	HUN
ICELAND 352	IS	ISL
INDIA 356	IN	IND

continues

Country Number	A 2 Code	A 3 Code
INDONESIA 360	ID	IDN
IRAN (ISLAMIC REPUBLIC OF) 364	IR	IRN
IRAQ 368	IQ	IRQ
IRELAND 372	IE	IRL
ISRAEL 376	IL	ISR
ITALY 380	IT	ITA
JAMAICA 388	JM	JAM
JAPAN 392	JP	JPN
JORDAN 400	JO	JOR
KAZAKHSTAN 398	KZ	KAZ
KENYA 404	KE	KEN
KIRIBATI 296	KI	KIR
KOREA, DEMOCRATIC PEOPLE'S REPUBLIC OF 408	KP	PRK
KOREA, REPUBLIC OF 410	KR	KOR
KUWAIT 414	KW	KWT
KYRGIZSTAN 417	KG	KGZ

Country Number	A 2 Code	A 3 Code
LAO PEOPLE'S DEMOCRATIC REPUBLIC 418	LA	LAO
LATVIA 428	LV	LVA
LEBANON 422	LB	LBN
LESOTHO 426	LS	LSO
LIBERIA 430	LR	LBR
LIBYAN ARAB JAMAHIRIYA 434	LY	LBY
LIECHTENSTEIN 438	LI	LIE
LITHUANIA 440	LT	LTU
LUXEMBOURG 442	LU	LUX
MACAU 446	MO	MAC
MADAGASCAR 450	MG	MDG
MALAWI 454	MW	MWI
MALAYSIA 458	MY	MYS
MALDIVES 462	MV	MDV
MALI 466	ML	MLI

continues

Country Number	A 2 Code	A 3 Code
MALTA 470	MT	MLT
MARSHALL ISLANDS 584	MH	MHL
MARTINIQUE 474	MQ	MTQ
MAURITANIA 478	MR	MRT
MAURITIUS 480	MU	MUS
MEXICO 484	MX	MEX
MICRONESIA 583	FM	FSM
MOLDOVA, REPUBLIC OF 498	MD	MDA
MONACO 492	MC	MCO
MONGOLIA 496	MN	MNG
MONTSERRAT 500	MS	MSR
MOROCCO 504	MA	MAR
MOZAMBIQUE 508	MZ	MOZ
MYANMAR 104	MM	MMR
NAMIBIA 516	NA	NAM
NAURU 520	NR	NRU
NEPAL 524	NP	NPL

Country Number	A 2 Code	A 3 Code
NETHERLANDS 528	NL	NLD
NETHERLANDS ANTILLES 532	AN	ANT
NEUTRAL ZONE 536	NT	NTZ
NEW CALEDONIA 540	NC	NCL
NEW ZEALAND 554	NZ	NZL
NICARAGUA 558	NI	NIC
NIGER 562	NE	NER
NIGERIA 566	NG	NGA
NIUE ISLAND 570	NU	NIU
NORFOLK ISLAND 574	NF	NFK
NORTHERN MARIANAS ISLANDS 580	MP	MNP
NORWAY 578	NO	NOR
OMAN 512	OM	OMN
PAKISTAN 586	PK	PAK
PALAU 585	PW	PLW
PANAMA 590	PA	PAN

continues

Country	A 2	A 3
Number	Code	Code
PAPUA NEW GUINEA 598	PG	PNG
PARAGUAY 600	PY	PRY
PERU 604	PE	PER
PHILIPPINES 608	PH	PHL
PITCAIRN ISLAND 612	PN	PCN
POLAND 616	PL	POL
PORTUGAL 620	PT	PRT
PUERTO RICO 630	PR	PRI
QATAR 634	QA	QAT
REUNION 638	RE	REU
ROMANIA 642	RO	ROM
RUSSIAN FEDERATION 643	RU	RUS
RWANDA 646	RW	RWA
ST. HELENA 654	SH	SHN
SAINT KITTS AND NEVIS 659	KN	KNA
SAINT LUCIA 662	LC	LCA
ST. PIERRE AND MIQUELON 666	PM	SPM

Country Number	A 2 Code	A 3 Code
SAINT VINCENT AND THE GRENADINES 670	VC	VCT
SAMOA 882	WS	WSM
SAN MARINO 674	SM	SMR
SAO TOME AND PRINCIPE 678	ST	STP
SAUDI ARABIA 682	SA	SAU
SENEGAL 686	SN	SEN
SEYCHELLES 690	SC	SYC
SIERRA LEONE 694	SL	SLE
SINGAPORE 702	SG	SGP
SLOVENIA (N/A)	SI	SVN
SOLOMON ISLANDS 090	SB	SLB
SOMALIA 706	SO	SOM
SOUTH AFRICA 710	ZA	ZAF
FORMER SOVIET UNION 810	SU	SUN
SPAIN 724	ES	ESP
SRI LANKA 144	LK	LKA

continues

Country Number	A 2 Code	A 3 Code
SUDAN 736	SD	SDN
SURINAME 740	SR	SUR
SVALBARD AND JAN MAYEN ISLANDS 744	SJ	SJM
SWAZILAND 748	SZ	SWZ
SWEDEN 752	SE	SWE
SWITZERLAND 756	CH	CHE
SYRIAN ARAB REPUBLIC 760	SY	SYR
TAIWAN, PROVINCE OF CHINA 158	TW	TWN
TAJIKISTAN 158	TJ	TJK
TANZANIA, UNITED REPUBLIC OF 834	TZ	TZA
THAILAND 764	TH	THA
TOGO 768	TG	TGO
TOKELAU 772	TK	TKL
TONGA 776	TO	TON
TRINIDAD AND TOBAGO 780	TT	TTO
TUNISIA 788	TN	TUN
TURKEY 792	TR	TUR

Country Number	A 2 Code	A 3 Code
TURKMENISTAN 795	TM	TKM
TURKS AND CAICOS ISLANDS 796	TC	TCA
TUVALU 798	TV	TUV
UGANDA 800	UG	UGA
UKRAINE 804	UA	UKR
UNITED ARAB EMIRATES 784	AE	ARE
UNITED KINGDOM 826	GB	GBR
UNITED STATES 840	US	USA
UNITED STATES MINOR OUTLYING ISLANDS 581	UM	UMI
URUGUAY 858	UY	URY
UZBEKISTAN 860	UZ	UZB
VANUATU 548	VU	VUT
VATICAN CITY STATE (HOLY SEE) 336	VA	VAT
VENEZUELA 862	VE	VEN
VIET NAM 704	VN	VNM

continues

Country Number	A 2 Code	A 3 Code
VIRGIN ISLANDS (BRITISH) 092	VG	VGB
VIRGIN ISLANDS (U.S.) 850	VI	VIR
WALLIS AND FUTUNA ISLANDS 876	WF	WLF
WESTERN SAHARA 732	EH	ESH
WESTERN SAMOA (SEE SAMOA)		
YEMEN, REPUBLIC OF 887	YE	YEM
YUGOSLAVIA 890	YU	YUG
ZAIRE 180	ZR	ZAR
ZAMBIA 894	ZM	ZMB
ZIMBABWE 716	ZW	ZWE

The Unofficial Smiley Dictionary

The following is a list of cute little characters that will accentuate your message while you're on the Internet.

:-) Your basic smiley. This smiley is used to inflect a sarcastic or joking statement since we can't hear voice inflection over the Internet.

;-) Winky smiley. User just made a flirtatious and/or sarcastic remark. More of a "don't hit me for what I just said" smiley.

:-(Frowning smiley. User did not like that last statement or is upset or depressed about something.

:-I Indifferent smiley. Better than a frowning smiley but not quite as good as a happy smiley.

:-> User just made a really biting sarcastic remark. Worse than a :-).

>:->	User just made a really devilish remark.
>;->	Winky and devil combined. A very lewd remark was just made.

Those are the basic ones... Here are some somewhat less common ones:

(-:	User is left handed
%-)	User has been staring at a green screen for 15 hours straight
:*)	User is drunk
[:]	User is a robot
7:^]	User is Ronald Reagan
8-)	User is wearing sunglasses
B:-)	Sunglasses on head
::-)	User wears normal glasses
B-)	User wears horn-rimmed glasses
8:-)	User is a little girl
:-{)	User has a mustache
:-{}	User wears lipstick
{:-)	User wears a toupee
}:-(	Toupee in an updraft
:-[	User is a Vampire

:-E	Bucktoothed vampire
:-F	Bucktoothed vampire with one tooth missing
:-7	User just made a wry statement
:-*	User just ate something sour
:-)~	User drools
:-~)	User has a cold
#-)	User is feeling no pain
#-(	User is hungover
:'-(	User is crying
:'-)	User is so happy, she/he is crying
:-@	User is screaming
:-#	User wears braces
:^)	User has a broken nose
:v)	User has a broken nose, but it's the other way
:_)	User's nose is sliding off of his face
:-&	User is tongue tied
=:-)	User is a hosehead
-:-)	User is a punk rocker
-:-(	(Real punk rockers don't smile)
:=)	User has two noses

':-)	User shaved one of his eyebrows off this morning
,:-)	Same thing... other side
I-I	User is asleep
I-O	User is yawning/snoring
:-Q	User is a smoker
:-?	User smokes a pipe
%\v	User is Picasso
O-)	Megaton Man on Patrol! (Or else, user is a scuba diver)
O :-)	User is an angel (at heart, at least)
:-P	Nyahhhh!
:-S	User just made an incoherent statement
:-D	User is laughing (at you!)
:-X	User's lips are sealed
:-C	User is really bummed
:-/	User is skeptical
C=:-)	User is a chef
8=:-)	User is a pastry chef
*<:-)	User is wearing a Santa Claus Hat
:-o	Uh-ohh!...
(8-o	...It's Mr. Bill!

*:o)	And Bozo the Clown!
8(:-)	Mouseketeer
3:]	Pet smiley
3:[	Mean pet smiley
=^)	User is Dagwood Bumstead
d8=	Your pet beaver is wearing goggles and a hard hat
E-:-)	User is a Ham radio operator
:-9	User is licking his/her lips
[:-)	User is wearing a walkman
(:I	User is an egghead
<:-I	User is a dunce
K:P	User is a little kid with a propeller beanie
:-0	No Yelling! (Quiet Lab)
:-:	Mutant Smiley
	The invisible smiley
8 :-)	User is a wizard
C=}>;*{))	Mega-Smiley... A drunk, devilish chef with a toupee in an updraft, a mustache, and a double chin

Note: A lot of these can be typed without noses to make midget smileys.

:)	Midget smiley

:]	Gleep... a friendly midget smiley who will gladly be your friend
=)	Tired but happy
:}	Sly little snake
:>	Bookworm
8)	Frogman
:@	User is in dentistry
:D	New baby
:I	Hmmm...
:(	Sad
:[	Real Downer
:<	User is in pain
:{	Fu manchu
:O	Yelling
:C	Feed the baby
:Q	Lollipop
:,(	Crying
[]	Hugs and...
:*	...Kisses
|I	Asleep
|^o	Snoring

:-'	Smiley spitting out its chewing tobacco
:-1	Contented smiley
:-!	Whispering
:-#l	Smiley face with bushy mustache
:-$	Smiley banker
:-%	Smiley face with its mouth wired shut
:-6	Smiley after eating something sour
:-7	Smiley after a wry statement
8-)	Smiley swimmer
:-*	Smiley after eating something bitter
:-0	Smiley orator
(:-(	Unsmiley frowning
(:-)	Smiley big-face
):-)	Smiley big-face, II
):-(	Unsmiley big-face
)8-)	Scuba smiley big-face
:-q	Smiley trying to touch its tongue to its nose
:-e	Disappointed smiley
:-t	Cross smiley
:-i	Semi-smiley

:-o	Smiley singing national anthem
:-p	Smiley sticking its tongue out (at you!)
:-[	Un-smiley blockhead
:-]	Smiley blockhead
:-{	Smiley variation on a theme
:-}	Ditto
{:-)	Smiley with its hair parted in the middle
}:-)	Windy day
:-a	Lefty smilely touching tongue to nose
:-s	Smiley after a BIZARRE comment
:-d	Lefty smiley razzing you
g-)	Smiley with pince-nez glasses
:-j	Left-smiling smiley
:-l	"Have an ordinary day" smiley
:-x	"My lips are sealed" smiley
:-c	Bummed out smiley
:-v	Talking head smiley
:-=)	Older smiley with mustache
}:^#})	Mega-smiley: updrafted, bushy-mustached, pointy nosed smiley with a double-chin
~~:-(	net.flame

I-)	Hee hee
O I-)	net.religion
I-D	Ho ho
:->	Hey hey
8 :-I	net.unix-wizards
:-(	Boo hoo
X-(	net.suicide
:-I	Hmm
E-:-I	net.ham-radio
:-O	Uh oh
>:-I	net.startrek
:-P	nyah nyah
3:o[	net.pets
I-P	yuk
:-}	beard
:-{	mustache
:-X	bow tie
8-)	glasses
B-)	horn-rims
8:-)	glasses on forehead

:-8(	condescending stare
>:-<	mad
Drama	**:-(**
Comedy	**:-)**
Surprise	**:-o**
Suspense	**8-|**
Birth	**|-O**
Death	**8-#**
Infinity	**8**

The whois Servers List

The following is a list of organizations that offer whois lists at
their servers. These whois servers act as a sort of "white pages"
directory of all the users at a particular organization or institution. For a more detailed discussion of how to take advantage of
this Internet feature, see the whois section in Chapter 5, "Finding Information on the Internet."

U.S. Corporations

Preferred server name	Associated institution
camb.com	Cambridge Computer Associates C=US
whois.pacbell.com	Pacific Bell C=US
wp.psi.com	Performance Systems International C=US
whois.sunquest.com	Sunquest Information Systems C=US

U.S. Educational Institutions

teetot.acusd.edu	University of San Diego C=US
ns.arizona.edu	University of Arizona C=US
ducserv.duc.auburn.edu	Auburn University C=US
whois.bates.edu	Bates College C=US
whois.berkeley.edu	University of California at Berkeley C=US
caltech.edu	California Institute of Technology C=US
horton.caltech.edu	California Institute of Technology C=US
csufres.csufresno.edu	California State University— Fresno C=US
csuhayward.edu	California State University— Hayward C=US
csus.edu	California State University— Sacramento C=US
whois.cwru.edu	Case Western Reserve University C=US
cc.fsu.edu	Florida State University C=US
gettysburg.edu	Gettysburg College C=US
gmu.edu	George Mason University C=US
whois.dfci.harvard.edu	Dana-Farber Cancer Institute C=US
indiana.edu	Indiana University C=US
kean.edu	Kean College C=US
acad.csv.kutztown.edu	Kutztown University C=US
whois.rsmas.miami.edu	University of Miami, Rosentiel School of Marine and Atmospheric Sciences C=US

mit.edu	Massachusetts Institute of Technology C=US
whois.msstate.edu	Mississippi State University C=US
vax2.winona.msus.edu	Minnesota State University—Winona C=US
nau.edu	Northern Arizona University C=US
whois.ncsu.edu	North Carolina State University C=US
nd.edu	University of Notre Dame C=US
earth.njit.edu	New Jersey Institute of Technology C=US
acfcluster.nyu.edu	New York University, Courant Institute C=US
sun1.mcsr.olemiss.edu	University of Mississippi C=US
austin.onu.edu	Ohio Northern University C=US
ph.orst.edu	Oregon State University C=US
osu.edu	Ohio State University C=US
whois.oxy.edu	Occidental College C=US
cs.rit.edu	Rochester Institute of Technology C=US
whois.cc.rochester.edu	University of Rochester C=US
whitepages.rutgers.edu	Rutgers University C=US
whois.sdsu.edu	San Diego State University C=US
sonoma.edu	Sonoma State University C=US
stanford.edu	Stanford University C=US
camis.stanford.edu	Stanford University C=US
hpp.stanford.edu	Stanford University C=US
stjohns.edu	St. John's University C=US
sunysb.edu	State University of New York, Stony Brook C=US

syr.edu	Syracuse University C=US
whois.bcm.tmc.edu	Baylor College of Medicine C=US
tstc.edu	Texas State Technical College C=US
directory.uakron.edu	University of Akron C=US
uc.edu	University of Cincinnati C=US
thor.ece.uc.edu	University of Cincinnati C=US
directory.ucdavis.edu	University of California at Davis C=US
uchicago.edu	University of Chicago C=US
oac.ucla.edu	University of California at Los Angeles C=US
whois.ucsb.edu	University of California at Santa Barbara C=US
ucsd.edu	University of California at San Diego C=US
weber.ucsd.edu	University of California at San Diego, Division of Social Sciences C=US
cgl.ucsf.edu	University of California at San Francisco, School of Pharmacy C=US
whois.eng.ufl.edu	University of Florida C=US
whois.uh.edu	University of Houston C=US
umbc.edu	University of Maryland, Baltimore County C=US
ub.umd.edu	University of Baltimore C=US
umd5.umd.edu	University of Maryland C=US
umn.edu	University of Minnesota C=US

ns.unl.edu	University of Nebraska at Lincoln C=US
whois.uoregon.edu	University of Oregon C=US
whois.upenn.edu	University of Pennsylvania C=US
whois.vims.edu	Virginia Institute of Marine Science C=US
whois.virginia.edu	University of Virginia C=US
whois.wfu.edu	Wake Forest University C=US
wisc.edu	University of Wisconsin C=US
wpi.wpi.edu	Worcester Polytechnic Institute C=US

U.S. Government Agencies

dirsvc.xosi.doe.gov	U.S. Department of Energy C=US
llnl.gov	Lawrence Livermore National Laboratory C=US
x500.arc.nasa.gov	NASA Ames Research Center C=US
x500.gsfc.nasa.gov	NASA Goddard Space Flight Center C=US
wp.nersc.gov	National Energy Research Supercomputer Center C=US
seda.sandia.gov	Sandia National Laboratories C=US

U.S. Military Agencies

whois.nic.ddn.mil	DDN Network Information Center C=US
whois.nrl.navy.mil	Naval Research Laboratory C=US

Network Sites

wp.es.net	Energy Sciences Network C=US
ds.internic.net	Network Solutions, Inc. (non-MILNET/non-POC) C=US
whois.internic.net	Network Solutions, Inc. C=US
pilot.njin.net	New Jersey Intercampus Network C=US
whois.ripe.net	Reseaux IP Europeans C=NL

Non-U.S. Sites

whois.wu-wien.ac.at	Wirtschaftsuniversitaet Wien C=AT
archie.au	Australian Academic and Research Network C=AU
whois.adelaide.edu.au	University of Adelaide C=AU
wp.adelaide.edu.au	University of Adelaide C=AU
deakin.edu.au	Deakin University C=AU
uwa.edu.au	University of Western Australia C=AU
sserve.cc.adfa.oz.au	University College, Australian Defense Force Academy C=AU
jethro.ucc.su.oz.au	University of Sydney C=AU
whois.doc.ca	Communications Canada (The Federal Department of Communications) C=CA
whois.queensu.ca	Queen's University, Kingston, Canada C=CA
whois.unb.ca	University of New Brunswick C=CA
panda1.uottawa.ca	University of Ottawa C=CA
whois.usask.ca	University of Saskatchewan C=CA

phys.uvic.ca	University of Victoria, Physics & Astronomy C=CA
whois.uwo.ca	University of Western Ontario C=CA
horton.yorku.ca	York University C=CA
nic.switch.ch	SWITCH Teleinformatics Services C=CH
dfnnoc.gmd.de	Gesellschaft fuer Mathematik und Datenverarbeitung C=DE
whois.th-darmstadt.de	Darmstadt University of Technology C=DE
whois.tu-chemnitz.de	Technische Universitaet Chemnitz C=DE
deins.informatik.uni-dortmund.de	University of Dortmund C=DE
whois.uni-c.dk	Danish Computing Centre for Research and Education C=DK
cs.hut.fi	Helsinki University of Technology C=FI
jyu.fi	Jyvaskyla University C=FI
vtt.fi	Technical Research Centre of Finland C=FI
whois.citilille.fr	CITI Lille - France C=FR
whois.univ-lyon1.fr	Universite Claude Bernard Lyon I C=FR
sangam.ncst.ernet.in	National Centre for Software Technology C=IN
isgate.is	Association of Research Networks in Iceland C=IS
dsa.nis.garr.it	GARR-NIS c/o CNR-CNUCE C=IT
whois.nis.garr.it	GARR-NIS c/o CNR-CNUCE C=IT
whois.cc.keio.ac.jp	Keio University C=JP

whois.nic.ad.jp	Japan Network Information Center C=JP
whois.tue.nl	Eindhoven University of Technology C=NL
cantsc.canterbury.ac.nz	University of Canterbury C=NZ
directory.vuw.ac.nz	Victoria University, Wellington C=NZ
waikato.ac.nz	Waikato University C=NZ
archie.inesc.pt	ınstituto de Engenharia de Sistemas e Computadores C=PT
chalmers.se	Chalmers University of Technology C=SE
whois.gd.chalmers.se	Gothenburg Universities' Computing Centre C=SE
kth.se	Royal Institute of Technology C=SE
sics.se	Swedish Institute of Computer Science C=SE
whois.sunet.se	SUNET (Swedish University Network) C=SE
whois.uakom.sk	SANET (WAN of Slovak academic institutions) C=SK
src.doc.ic.ac.uk	Imperial College C=GB
nri.reston.va.us	Corporation for National Research Initiatives, Knowbot interface C=US
hippo.ru.ac.za	Rhodes University, Grahamstown C=ZA
whois.und.ac.za	University of Natal (Durban) C=ZA

INDEX

Riding the Internet Highway
REGISTRATION CARD

Fill out this card to receive information about future New Riders Publishing titles!

Name _____ **Title** _____

Company _____

Address _____

City/State/ZIP _____

I bought this book because _____
_____

I purchased this book from: **I purchase this many**
☐ A bookstore (Name _____)   **computer books**
☐ A software or electronics store (Name _____) **each year:**
☐ A mail order (Name of Catalog _____)   ☐ 1–5   ☐ 5 or more

I currently use these applications: _____
_____
_____
_____

I found these chapters to be the most informative: _____
_____

I found these chapters to be the least informative: _____
_____

Additional comments: _____
_____

☐ I would like to see my name in print! You may use my name and quote me in future New Riders products and promotions. My daytime phone number is: _____

New Riders Publishing 11711 North College Avenue • P.O. Box 90 • Carmel, Indiana 46032 USA

Fold Here

New Riders Publishing
11711 North College Avenue
P.O. Box 90
Carmel, Indiana 46032
USA

PLACE
STAMP
HERE

OPERATING SYSTEMS

INSIDE MS-DOS 6

MARK MINASI

A complete tutorial and reference!

MS-DOS 6
ISBN: 1-56205-132-6
$39.95 USA

DOS FOR NON-NERDS

MICHAEL GROH

Understanding this popular operating system is easy with this humorous, step-by-step tutorial.

Through DOS 6.0
ISBN: 1-56205-151-2
$18.95 USA

INSIDE SCO UNIX

STEVE GLINES, PETER SPICER, BEN HUNSBERGER, & KAREN WHITE

Everything users need to know to use the UNIX operating system for everyday tasks.

SCO Xenix 286, SCO Xenix 386, SCO UNIX/System V 386
ISBN: 1-56205-028-1
$29.95 USA

INSIDE SOLARIS SunOS

KARLA SAARI, KITA LONG, STEVEN R. LEE, & PAUL MARZIN

Comprehensive tutorial and reference to SunOS!

SunOS, Sun's version of UNIX for the SPARC workstation version 2.0
ISBN: 1-56205-032-X
$29.95 USA

NETWORKING TITLES

#1 Bestseller!

INSIDE NOVELL NETWARE, SPECIAL EDITION

DEBRA NIEDERMILLER-CHAFFINS & BRIAN L. CHAFFINS

This best-selling tutorial and reference has been updated and made even better!

NetWare 2.2 & 3.11

ISBN: 1-56205-096-6

$34.95 USA

MAXIMIZING NOVELL NETWARE

JOHN JERNEY & ELNA TYMES

Complete coverage of Novell's flagship product...for NetWare system administrators!

NetWare 3.11

ISBN: 1-56205-095-8

$39.95 USA

NETWARE: THE PROFESSIONAL REFERENCE, SECOND EDITION

KARANJIT SIYAN

This updated version for professional NetWare administrators and technicians provides the most comprehensive reference available for this phenomenal network system.

NetWare 2.2 & 3.11

ISBN: 1-56205-158-X

$42.95 USA

NETWARE 4: PLANNING AND IMPLEMENTATION

SUNIL PADIYAR

A guide to planning, installing, and managing a NetWare 4.0 network that serves the company's best objectives.

NetWare 4.0

ISBN: 1-56205-159-8

$27.95 USA

To Order, Call 1-800-428-5331

GRAPHICS TITLES

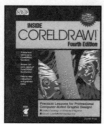

INSIDE CORELDRAW! 4.0, SPECIAL EDITION

DANIEL GRAY

An updated version of the #1 best-selling tutorial on CorelDRAW!

CorelDRAW! 4.0

ISBN: 1-56205-164-4

$34.95 USA

CORELDRAW! NOW!

NEW RIDERS PUBLISHING

The graphics approach to using CorelDRAW!

CorelDRAW! 2.01 & 3.0

ISBN: 1-56205-131-8

$21.95 USA

Coming Soon

CORELDRAW! SPECIAL EFFECTS

NEW RIDERS PUBLISHING

An inside look at award-winning techniques from professional CorelDRAW! designers!

CorelDRAW! 4.0

ISBN: 1-56205-123-7

$39.95 USA

INSIDE CORELDRAW! FOURTH EDITION

DANIEL GRAY

The popular tutorial approach to learning CorelDRAW!...with complete coverage of version 3.0!

CorelDRAW! 3.0

ISBN: 1-56205-106-7

$34.95 USA

To Order, Call 1-800-428-5331

Become a CNE with Help from a Pro!

The NetWare Training Guides are specifically designed and authored to help you prepare for the **Certified NetWare Engineer** exam.

NetWare Training Guide: Managing NetWare Systems

This book clarifies the CNE testing process and provides hints on how best to prepare for the CNE examinations. NetWare Training Guide: Managing NetWare Systems covers the following sections of the CNE exams:

- NetWare v 2.2 System Manager

- NetWare v 2.2 Advanced System Manager

- NetWare v 3.X System Manager

- NetWare v 3.X Advanced System Manager

ISBN: 1-56205-069-9, **$59.95 USA**

NetWare Training Guide: Networking Technology

This book covers more advanced topics and prepares you for the tough hardware and service/support exams. The following course materials are covered:

- MS-DOS

- Microcomputer Concepts

- Service and Support

- Networking Technologies

ISBN: 1-56205-145-8, **$59.95 USA**

DATE DUE

JUL 10 '95			
6-3 99			
OCT 2 7 1999		WITHDRAWN	